THE YOUNG PEOPLE'S
ENCYCLOPEDIA
OF THE
UNITED STATES

THE YOUNG PEOPLE'S

ENCYCLOPEDIA
OF THE
UNITED STATES

General Editor: William E. Shapiro

VOLUME 5: HESSIANS / LAWS

The Millbrook Press
Brookfield, Connecticut

First published in 1992 by The Millbrook Press Inc.,
2 Old New Milford Road, Brookfield, Connecticut 06804

© Grisewood & Dempsey Ltd. and The Millbrook Press Inc., 1992

LIBRARY OF CONGRESS CATALOGING-IN-PUBLICATION DATA

The Young People's Encyclopedia of the United States
p. cm.
Includes index.
Summary: A multivolume encyclopedia with over 1200 alphabetically-
arranged entries covering such topics as the history,
physical features, festivals, and music of the United States
and its neighbors, Mexico and Canada.
ISBN 1–56294–151–8
1. The United States—Encyclopedias. Juvenile.
2. North America—Encyclopedias. Juvenile.
[1. United States—Encyclopedias. 2. North America—Encyclopedias.]
E156.Y68 1992
970.003—dc 20   91–4141
                                                      CIP
                                                      AC

Printed in Italy
Bound in the United States

THE SUBJECT SYMBOLS

Each entry in this encyclopedia has its own easily recognized symbol opposite the heading. This symbol tells you at a glance which area of interest the entry falls into. Below are the 12 subject areas we have used. At the back of the work there is a list of all the articles divided into subject areas.

HISTORY Events from before colonial times to the present day.

LITERATURE AND THE ARTS Novelists, playwrights, folklore, folk art and crafts, theater, dance, painting, sculpture, architecture of the United States.

PEOPLE AND CULTURE Native and immigrant peoples of North America, their languages and customs, education, health and welfare, social issues.

GEOGRAPHY The land and climate of North America: geographic regions, mountain ranges, rivers and lakes, coastlines, national parks.

SCIENCE AND SPACE Explorations into fields of science and astronomy, famous scientists and innovators.

INDUSTRY AND TECHNOLOGY Transportation, natural resources, manufacturing — industries of yesterday and today.

GOVERNMENT AND LAW The U.S. government, its branches and how it works; the armed services and other governmental organizations; political parties; laws and treaties.

RELIGION, PHILOSOPHY, AND MYTH The wide variety of religious denominations, philosophers and their ideas, myths and legends.

SPORTS AND PASTIMES Baseball, football, basketball, and other sports, sports heroes, plus many hobbies.

COUNTRIES AND PLACES Our neighbors in North and Central America and places of interest.

ANIMALS, PLANTS, AND FOOD North American animals and their habitats, North American plants, agriculture and food, including regional specialities.

STATES AND CITIES Descriptions of each U.S. state, major cities, and sites within and around the country.

INDIAN handicrafts can chronicle a tribe's history, as seen on this detail of a Navajo Yei blanket.

HESSIANS

Hessians were German soldiers hired to aid the British during the American REVOLUTION. They were called Hessians because many of them came from the German province of Hesse-Kassel. Hessians fought in many European conflicts and were respected as fighters. But their defeat by General George WASHINGTON at the Battle of Trenton, New Jersey, on December 29, 1776, helped give the new American Army confidence. Many Hessians had no love for the British cause and either deserted or switched sides to fight with the colonists.

▲ American cartoonists often portrayed the Hessian soldiers as clowns because of their uniforms and their difficulty with the English language.

◄ Hiawatha was able to convince other Iroquois tribes to unite in 1570 because they all felt threatened by the Algonquins.

HIAWATHA

Hiawatha was a MOHAWK Indian leader who lived in the 1500s in what is now northern New York State. He and his teacher, Deganawidah, a Huron, founded the IROQUOIS LEAGUE. It included the Cayugas, Mohawks, Oneidas, Onondagas, and Senecas. This pact ended war among the Iroquois tribes and enabled them to fight off the Algonquins. In 1855, Henry Wadsworth LONGFELLOW wrote *The Song of Hiawatha*. The Indian in this poem was not based on the real Hiawatha.

▼ Frontiersmen agreed that Wild Bill Hickok was the "fastest gun in the West." He always carried two pearl-handled pistols.

HICKOK, James "Wild Bill"

Despite his lawless nickname, James Butler Hickok (1837–1876) was a U.S. marshal. Hickok was born in Illinois but later moved to Kansas. During the Civil War

▲ *The Flamingo Hotel is a Las Vegas landmark. The Hilton chain has hotels in 38 countries.*

he served as a scout and spy for the Union Army. He later became an Indian fighter.

As U.S. marshal of several Kansas frontier towns, he was responsible for keeping law and order. Hickok was known for his courage. On one occasion he fought a notorious gang single-handedly, killing three of them.

In 1872, Hickok displayed his legendary marksmanship in Buffalo Bill's Wild West Show. He was killed in a poker game by someone who shot him from behind.

HILTON, Conrad

Conrad Hilton (1887–1979) was America's most famous HOTEL owner. He became known as the "king of the innkeepers." He was born in San Antonio, New Mexico. Part of his house was used as a small hotel, so young Conrad learned many things about running hotels. In 1919 he bought his own hotel, the Mobley, in Cisco, Texas. It was successful and he was able to use the money he made to buy more hotels. By 1966, Hilton owned more than 60 hotels in the United States. These included the Waldorf-Astoria in New York City and the Beverly Hilton in Beverly Hills, California.

HISPANIC-AMERICANS

The U.S. Hispanic population is more than 24 million. This represents approximately 10 percent of the total U.S. population. The United States has the fifth largest Hispanic population in the world.

Hispanic-Americans can trace their origins to almost every Spanish-speaking country in the world. The largest group is Mexican-American (58.9 percent), followed by Puerto Rican (10.2 percent), Cuban (6.2 percent), and Central and South America (20.3 percent).

About 90 percent of Hispanic-Americans live in just nine states. Most live in California (36 percent), Texas (20 percent), New York (10 percent), and Florida (16 percent). The states of Illinois, Arizona, New Jersey, New Mexico, and Colorado also have large Hispanic populations.

Hispanic-Americans tend to have the same religious beliefs. The majority are Roman Catholics. They share several other characteristics as well. For example, they are younger and have larger families than the U.S. population as a

Famous Hispanic-Americans
Toney Anaya was governor of New Mexico from 1983 to 1987.
Romana Bañuelos was treasurer of the United States from 1971 to 1974.
Cesar Chavez organized California grape pickers in the 1960s.
Gloria Estefan is one of the world's most popular singers.
Lee Trevino has been a professional golf star for more than 25 years.
Fernando Valenzuela won baseball's Cy Young Award as the National League's best pitcher in 1981.

whole. It is estimated that Hispanic Americans will be the number one minority in the United States by the year 2015.

▲ *Hispanic-American children have the advantage of a dual culture—Spanish language and traditions in the United States.*

HISTORY OF CANADA *See* Canadian History

HISTORY OF THE UNITED STATES *See* American History

HOLIDAY, Billie

Billie Holiday (1915–1959) was a famous JAZZ singer. She was born in Baltimore and spent her early years in poverty. Her voice had a haunting, emotional quality. She worked through the 1930s and 1940s and made many recordings. Her work is still popular, and her records are collector's items. Holiday's personal life was tragic. She had a number of unhappy relationships. She became so dependent on drugs that her voice was affected and her career was ruined. Holiday wrote the story of her life and called it *Lady Sings the Blues*. This was the title of a film about her life made in 1972.

HOLIDAYS

A holiday is a day celebrating a certain event or occasion or honoring a famous person. The word comes from "holy day" and indicates that holidays were origi-

Federal Holidays
New Year's Day (January 1)
Martin Luther King, Jr., Day (3rd Monday in January)
George Washington's Birthday, or Presidents' Day (3rd Monday in February)
Memorial Day (last Monday in May)
Independence Day (July 4)
Labor Day (1st Monday in September)
Columbus Day (2nd Monday in October)
Veterans' Day (November 11)
Thanksgiving Day (4th Thursday in November)
Christmas Day (December 25)

▲ Independence Day celebrations on July 4 had already become a tradition by 1812.

nally religious in nature. In the United States few people work on Sunday, for example, because Christians consider it the Sabbath day. Christmas is a legal holiday in all states. Other legal holidays, such as Independence Day or George Washington's birthday, are meant to remind people of the American past. Schools, public offices, and most private businesses are closed on these days. The president and Congress declare legal holidays for the District of Columbia, the federal territories, and federal employees. Each of the states, however, decides what will be a legal holiday within its borders.

▼ The "Hollywood" sign was built in 1922 and restored in 1978. Each letter is 45 feet (14 m) high.

HOLLYWOOD

Hollywood is regarded as the center of the motion picture industry. It is a district of LOS ANGELES, Cali-

fornia. In the early 1900s, moviemakers discovered how well suited southern California was to making motion pictures. It had a sunny climate, varied scenery, and a large labor market. The first studio was built in 1911. The early motion pictures were silent films. In the late 1920s, the first sound films were produced. Now many of the studios are used for making television films.

HOLMES, Oliver Wendell

Oliver Wendell Holmes (1809–1894) was a physician, university professor, poet, novelist, and essayist. Holmes came from a prominent Boston family. He received his medical degree from Harvard in 1836. After practicing medicine for ten years, he taught medicine and later became dean of the Harvard Medical School.

Holmes was the author of such popular poems as "Old Ironsides" and "The Chambered Nautilus." He also wrote three novels, including *Elsie Venner*. For the *Atlantic Monthly* he wrote a series of essays in the form of witty conversations around an imaginary breakfast table. Twelve of these essays were published as *The Autocrat of the Breakfast-Table* in 1858.

HOLMES, Oliver Wendell, Jr.

Oliver Wendell Holmes, Jr. (1841–1935), had at least as distinguished a career as his father. He was a lawyer, legal historian, philosopher, and a justice of the U.S. Supreme Court for nearly 30 years.

Holmes obtained his law degree from Harvard Law School in 1866. While practicing law, he also wrote and lectured on it. His book *The Common Law* expressed his belief that the law should grow out of the experiences of society. It should not, he said, be considered a fixed, absolute system.

After serving as a justice and chief justice on the Massachusetts Supreme Court, Holmes was appointed to the U.S. Supreme Court in 1902. He was, and still is, considered one of the great legal minds of his age.

HOMER, Winslow

Winslow Homer (1836–1910) was one of America's greatest painters. He began painting scenes of country life. Many of these paintings were used in the magazine

Hollywood now produces far more television movies, series, and commercials than it does motion pictures. In the golden age of Hollywood, a major studio such as MGM had a lot the size of a small town. It included studio offices, film laboratories, thousands of expensive costumes, prop-making shops, vast outdoor sets, editing rooms, restaurants, and many sound stages.

▲ *Oliver Wendell Holmes, Jr., continued giving lectures and publishing until he was in his eighties.*

The Cooper-Hewitt Museum in New York City contains the largest collection of Winslow Homer drawings in the world.

▲ *Winslow Homer's* Snap the Whip, *painted in 1872, captured the innocence of children playing in a New England meadow.*

Harper's Weekly. Homer's paintings became famous in Europe and he lived in England from 1881 to 1882. There he began painting pictures of the sea. When he returned to the United States, he lived in Maine and painted scenes of that state's seacoast. Homer's paintings were very realistic. He said, "When I have selected the thing carefully, I paint exactly what appears." Two of his best paintings are *The Northeaster* and *Cannon Rock.*

HOMESTEAD ACT

One of the largest movements west in U.S. history occurred in 1889. The government opened up 2 million acres (800,000 ha) of former Indian land in the Oklahoma Territory for settlement. As soon as the starting gun was fired on April 22, thousands of homesteaders raced to claim the land. By sunset all the land was gone. Those homesteaders who jumped the gun were called "Sooners," still a nickname for Oklahomans.

The Homestead Act was passed in 1862. It followed decades of pressure on Congress by the homestead movement. The people in this movement said that public land belonged to the people, and that the head of every family should be given a small farm, or homestead. Southerners opposed the Homestead Act. They feared that free land would lead to the creation of nonslave states. The Homestead Act was passed by Congress only after the Southern states seceded from the Union and the CIVIL WAR began.

The act of 1862 offered 160 acres (65 ha) of land in what is now the Midwest for a small fee to anyone who would occupy and cultivate it for five years. By 1900, as many as 600,000 homesteads were awarded. Many of the settlers failed, through lack of experience, to make a success of their farms. But others prospered, and the North's harvests increased dramatically as a result.

HOOVER, Herbert

Herbert Clark Hoover was the 31st president of the United States. The worst DEPRESSION in U.S. history occurred during his presidency. Before he left office, one out of every four wage earners was out of work.

Hoover was an engineer and businessman before entering public affairs. During and after World War I, his relief work in Europe kept millions of people from starving to death. From 1921 to 1928 he was secretary of commerce under President Warren G. HARDING.

With the election of Hoover, a Republican, in 1928, the country expected the prosperity of the previous years to continue. But in October 1929, prices on the New York Stock Exchange, which had reached record

levels, suddenly dropped. Soon businesses all over the United States were closing in record numbers.

Under Hoover's direction, the federal government provided loans to banks and other firms, home owners, and farmers. He supported public works and conservation programs. But he refused to support government "handouts" such as federal aid to those out of work. Hoover felt that help for the poor should come from charities, private companies, and state and local governments. By 1933, 13 million Americans were out of work. Many people lost their homes and became squatters living in shantytowns known as Hoovervilles.

Most Americans felt that Hoover had not done enough to end the Depression. As a result, he lost the 1932 election to Franklin D. ROOSEVELT. In retirement, Hoover headed commissions that proposed ways to make the federal government more efficient.

▲ *Public confidence in banks hit an all-time low during President Hoover's administration. By the end of 1932 more than 5,000 banks had gone out of business.*

Herbert Hoover
Born: August 10, 1874, in West Branch, Iowa
Education: Stanford University
Political party: Republican
Term of office: 1929–1933
Married: 1899 to Lou Henry
Died: October 20, 1964, in New York City

▲ J. Edgar Hoover set up an efficient anticrime organization, but he was accused of neglecting the civil rights of many suspects.

HOOVER, J. Edgar

J. Edgar Hoover (1895–1972) was head of the FEDERAL BUREAU OF INVESTIGATION (FBI) for 48 years. He served under every president from Calvin Coolidge to Richard Nixon. Hoover was born in Washington, D.C. After becoming a lawyer, he took a job with the U.S. Department of Justice. Just seven years later he was made director of the FBI, the branch of the Justice Department that investigated federal crimes. When Hoover took charge of it, it was badly run. Hoover changed it into a strong and effective organization. He set up the FBI National Academy at Quantico, Virginia, and established the FBI Laboratory. Under Hoover, the FBI waged a war against organized crime in the 1930s. And during World War II, it captured many foreign spies. However, Hoover became obsessed with power and his ability to influence people and events. He became one of the most powerful people in the nation. It was only after his death in 1972 that Congress revealed that Hoover had abused his power.

HOPI

The Hopi are an INDIAN tribe of the southwestern United States. Their name comes from the word *hopitu*, which means "the peaceful ones." They are descended from an ancient Indian people called the Anasazi, who came to the area around 1000 B.C. The Hopi are farmers, and their religion is tied to their environment. Religious ceremonies are centered around the growing cycle of maize, or corn. Winter is considered the most sacred season. At this time ceremonies are held using the kachina doll. These dolls are made of wood and horsehair and represent spirits. Today about 8,000 Hopi live on a reservation in Arizona.

▲ Kachina dolls represent Hopi gods who live in a mysterious country hidden in neighboring mountains.

HOPPER, Edward

Edward Hopper (1882–1967) was one of the greatest American painters of this century. His paintings are realistic and use ordinary settings such as bedrooms, city streets, and empty theaters as their subjects. Many of them show the sadness of everyday life. *Nighthawks*, for example, shows what seem to be lonely people late at night in a mostly empty diner. His paintings contain no

◄ *In paintings such as Pennsylvania Coal Town, Edward Hopper showed his feeling for people and places that other artists ignored.*

unnecessary details to distract from the real subject of the painting. *Cape Cod Afternoon* is typical of his later work. He began to observe nature with the same attention he gave to his city works.

HORSE RACING

In the United States, horse racing is the best attended of any sporting event. In *flat racing*, jockeys ride Thoroughbred horses around a flat track. The most famous flat race is the 1¼-mile (2-km) KENTUCKY DERBY. Horses that win the Kentucky Derby, Belmont Stakes, and Preakness Stakes win the Triple Crown.

In *harness racing*, the horse pulls a driver in a sulky, a two-wheeled carriage. Important harness races take place at Yonkers Raceway, in New York, and Meadowlands Raceway, in New Jersey. Standardbred horses are used for harness racing.

Triple Crown Winners (Kentucky Derby, Preakness, and Belmont Stakes)	
1978	Affirmed
1977	Seattle Slew
1973	Secretariat
1948	Citation
1946	Assault
1943	Count Fleet
1941	Whirlaway
1937	War Admiral
1935	Omaha
1930	Gallant Fox
1919	Sir Barton

◄ *Harness racing developed in the United States in the 1700s. Most modern harness trotters (a type of racehorse) are descendants of Hambletonian, a famous 19th-century trotter.*

325

▶ *Some Plains Indian tribes, such as the Cheyenne and Pawnee, quickly learned how to tame and ride horses for hunting and war.*

Special Horse Terms

Bronco: an untamed horse in the American West

Colt: a male horse less than four years old

Filly: a female horse less than four years old

Hand: unit of measurement (4 in, or 10 cm) used to determine a horse's height

Mare: a female horse more than four years old

Mustang: a wild horse on the western plains

HORSES AND THEIR RELATIVES

The United States has a number of unique breeds of horses. All are descended from the horses of the Europeans. The Morgan is one of the most popular. Small but strong, it was once used as a harness horse and now makes a good saddle horse.

The quarter horse is the fastest horse over a short distance. Originally the horse was bred for quarter

races, which were a quarter of a mile long. Some quarter horses are still raced today because they can start, stop, and turn quickly. They are also used for ranch work and as polo ponies.

The Appaloosa was originally bred from mustangs (wild horses) in the Palouse River region of Idaho by the Nez Percé Indians. It is an excellent saddle horse.

The American saddle horse is a high-stepping show horse. The Tennessee walking horse is known for its steady running walk, which makes it comfortable to ride. The standardbred horse, also called the American trotting horse, is used in harness racing. Today, thousands of wild horses, or mustangs, roam the open spaces of the West. They are descended from horses that escaped captivity a hundred or more years ago.

Donkeys are small, sturdy, surefooted relatives of horses. They are used for riding, pulling carts, or carrying loads. Small donkeys, or burros, are used as pack animals. The offspring of a male donkey (jackass) and a female horse (mare) is a mule. It is as large as a horse but has long ears and is stronger and more surefooted. Mules cannot usually reproduce. In the United States nearly all mules are used on farms, especially in the southern states.

HOTELS AND MOTELS

Hotels and motels serve people who travel and need a temporary place to stay.

Hotels developed from inns, which provided food, entertainment, and a place to sleep for travelers. The first American inn was built in Jamestown, Virginia, in 1610. The first building to be designed as a hotel was the City Hotel in New York City. It was built in the late 1700s. Motels, in which rooms can be reached directly from a parking area, developed later, along with automobile travel.

Today the largest hotels may have as many as 3,000 rooms. These are usually resort hotels, such as those by the seashore, that attract many tourists. Often hotels and motels are part of a chain.

▲ *The Breakers Hotel in Palm Beach, California, shows the splendor of hotels that were modeled on the European tradition.*

HOUDINI, Harry

Harry Houdini (1874–1926) was a famous magician. He was known especially for his death-defying escapes. Houdini's real name was Ehrich Weiss. Soon after he was born in Budapest, Hungary, his family moved to Appleton, Wisconsin. During his early career, Houdini performed simple magic tricks with cards. But while doing this to earn a living, he perfected the escape techniques that made him world famous. Houdini broke free from locked trunks sealed with chains. He astounded his audience by one of his most dangerous acts: escaping from a tank that was completely filled with water and in which he was hanging upside down.

▼ *Posters for Harry Houdini's performances always showed the types of locks and handcuffs that he had mastered.*

HOUSE OF REPRESENTATIVES

The House of Representatives is the lower house of the CONGRESS of the United States. The other house is the SENATE. Both meet in the CAPITOL, in Washington, D.C. The first House of Representatives, which met in 1789 in New York City, the nation's first capital, had 65 representatives. Since 1911 there have been 435 representatives. They are elected every two years. The number of representatives from each state is determined by that state's population according to the most recent CENSUS. After the 1990 census, the fast-growing states of the South and West gained many House seats.

Members of the House of Representatives must be

States with Most Representatives	
California	52
New York	31
Texas	30
Florida	23
Pennsylvania	21
Illinois	20
Ohio	19
Michigan	16
New Jersey	14
North Carolina	12
Georgia	11
Massachusetts	11
Virginia	11
Indiana	10

residents of the state from which they are chosen. They must be 25 years old or older. And they must have been U.S. citizens for at least seven years.

The speaker of the House presides over sessions and appoints members of important committees. The speaker is a member of the party—Democratic or Republican—that has the most seats in the House.

HOUSING

From the time of the first settlers, Americans have dreamed of owning their own home. Today there are more than 93 million housing units in the United States. About two thirds of them are owned by the people who live in them. These include detached houses, condominiums, and cooperative apartments. Still, many millions of people live in rented apartments and houses.

Between 4 million and 5 million homes are sold each year. The average cost of a new house passed $100,000 in 1987. Affordable housing has become an important concern. The U.S. Department of Housing and Urban Development supplies billions of dollars in loans each year. This money is used to build low-cost housing.

HOUSTON

Houston is the largest city in TEXAS, and the fourth largest in the country, with a population of 1,630,553. It was founded in 1836 and named after General Sam HOUSTON, hero of the Texan war of independence from Mexico. The city began to grow quickly in the early 1900s when oil was discovered nearby. It is an important port, manufacturing and transportation center, as well. The Houston Ship Canal connects the city with the Gulf of Mexico. In the 1960s, NASA built the Manned Spacecraft Center southeast of the city. It was later renamed the Lyndon B. Johnson Space Center.

HOUSTON, Samuel

Sam Houston (1793–1863) was a giant of American history. He was a military hero, a U.S. representative and senator, the first president of the Republic of Texas, and the governor of both Tennessee and Texas.

Houston grew up on a farm in Tennessee. While in his teens, he lived with the Cherokee Indians, who

▲ Houston's modern skyline is reflected in the Buffalo Bayou, which flows through the center of the city.

called him Black Raven. After the WAR OF 1812, Houston studied law and began to build a career in politics. He was elected to Congress from Tennessee in 1823 and was elected governor four years later. In 1829, however, Houston resigned and once again went live with the Cherokees, who adopted him into the tribe.

In 1832, President Andrew JACKSON sent Houston on a special mission to Texas, which was then part of Mexico. American settlers revolted against Mexican rule in 1835. A year later Houston was made commander of the Texas army and in the Battle of San Jacinto, he and his troops, outnumbered two to one, defeated the Mexicans. Texas became independent, and Houston became the first president of the Republic of Texas.

Texas became the 28th state of the Union in 1845, and Houston was elected U.S. senator. He became governor in 1859. Just before the start of the CIVIL WAR in 1861, Texas seceded from the Union and joined the Confederacy. Houston opposed this and was forced out of office. He died two years later.

▲ Sam Houston had the distinction of being elected governor of the states of Tennessee and Texas.

Sam Houston, famous as one of the founders of independent Texas, grew up with Cherokees and went through tests to become a tribe member. He promised equal rights for Cherokees and other tribes when he became president of Texas in 1848. These freedoms were taken away two years later when his term of office ended.

HOWE, Elias

Elias Howe (1819–1867) invented the sewing machine. He patented it in 1846, sold an English company the British rights to the machine and moved to England so that he could improve the design. In 1849, Howe returned to the United States. His machine had not done well in England and he was now very poor. He soon found that Isaac SINGER and others had manufactured and sold sewing machines based on his invention. Howe sued them and won. After years of poverty, Howe became a rich man.

▼ Elias Howe's sewing machine was operated by hand. Later sewing machines used pedals and finally electricity.

HOWE, Julia Ward

Julia Ward Howe (1819–1910) was a writer and social reformer. She and her husband, Samuel Gridley Howe, published the ABOLITIONIST newspaper the *Commonwealth* in Boston. Early in the Civil War she wrote "The Battle Hymn of the Republic." Set to the tune of "John Brown's Body," this stirring song became the favorite war song of the Union Army. After the war and the freeing of the slaves, she fought to get women the right to vote. She was the first president of the New England Woman Suffrage Association.

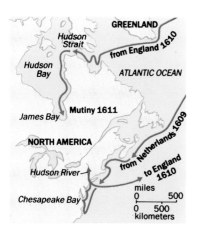

▲ *Henry Hudson's explorations helped set the stage for English and Dutch colonization.*

HUBBLE, Edwin

Edwin Powell Hubble (1889–1953) was one of the greatest astronomers of this century. He studied galaxies, distant bodies of stars like our Milky Way. By measuring their spectra (the colors in their light), he was able to tell how fast their distance from us was changing. In 1924 he announced that his measurements showed that the farther apart two galaxies are, the faster they tend to be moving away from one another. This became known as Hubble's Law. It led some astronomers to a theory that the universe began billions of years ago at a single point with a great explosion called the "Big Bang." The resulting matter is still expanding outward at enormous speeds in all directions.

HUDSON, Henry

The English explorer Henry Hudson (?–1611) made four voyages to the Arctic and North America. He was searching for a northern sea route between Europe and Asia. The HUDSON RIVER, Hudson Bay, and Hudson Strait are named for him.

Hudson made his first voyage in 1607. He reached the east coast of Greenland but turned back after coming upon huge ice floes. A second attempt in 1608 also failed to find the Northwest Passage. In the following year, Hudson sailed with a crew of 20 men aboard his ship, the *Half Moon*. He explored the Atlantic coast of North America as far south as present-day North Carolina. He then traveled far up the river. The river was later named after him.

Hudson's last voyage was in 1610. He sailed through Hudson Strait into Hudson Bay. It soon became ice clogged, and he had to spend the winter there. In the following spring, when the ice melted, his crew mutinied. Hudson, his son, and several others were set adrift in a small boat. They were never heard from again.

▲ *The source of the Hudson River is in the Adirondack region, one of the least populated areas of New York State. But its mouth, in New York City, is one of the busiest waterways in the world.*

HUDSON RIVER

The Hudson River is 306 miles (492 km) long. It rises in the ADIRONDACK MOUNTAINS in Lake Tear-of-the-Clouds, in New York State. The river flows south into New York Bay, the large natural harbor at New York

City. The Italian Giovanni da VERRAZANO discovered New York Bay and the mouth of the river in 1524. (The Verrazano-Narrows Bridge is named after him.) The Hudson River itself was first explored in 1609 by the English navigator Henry HUDSON, who was working for the Dutch. The Hudson is an important route for travel and trade. Robert FULTON's steamships began to carry passengers on the Hudson in 1807.

During the 1800s the Hudson's Bay Company was the only source of goods for many Canadians.

HUDSON'S BAY COMPANY

The Hudson's Bay Company was founded in 1670. Its original purpose was to search for a Northwest Passage to the Pacific Ocean and to establish a fur trade in the lands surrounding Hudson Bay.

For a short time in the early 1800s, the company held a monopoly on the fur trade. It ruled a vast territory in Canada that stretched from the Atlantic Ocean to the Pacific. In 1870 it was required to sell most of its holding to the newly created Dominion of Canada. Today the company is still one of the world's leading fur traders, and it owns many retail stores.

HUGHES, (James) Langston

The poetry and prose of Langston Hughes (1902–1967) are among the most eloquent expressions of what it is to be black in a white-dominated society.

Hughes published his first collection of poems, *The Weary Blues*, in 1926, to an enthusiastic reception. Among his many other books are a collection of short stories, *The Ways of White Folks*, and *A Pictorial History of the Negro in America*, which was written for children. The poems in *The Panther and the Lash* are concerned with the militant black movements of the 1960s. In *The Big Sea*, Hughes told the story of his life up to the age of 28. *Simple Speaks His Mind* and *The Best of Simple* are collections of humorous sketches.

▼ *Langston Hughes found respect as a writer early on, but his struggle as a black American continued all his life.*

▼ *The hummingbird's long, hollow tongue darts in and out of its beak. It is forked to help the bird collect nectar.*

Ruby-throated hummingbird

HUMMINGBIRD

Hummingbirds include the smallest BIRDS in the world. They get their name from the sound their wings make. The birds fly very fast. Like a helicopter, they can fly up or down or forward, backward, or sideways. And they can hover in one place. They hover over plants to feed

▲ *Some Huron tomahawks could also be used as peace pipes. Other tribes agreed that Huron tobacco was the best.*

on nectar from flowers and also insects.

These small, brightly colored birds live only in the New World, mostly in Latin America. The smallest in the United States is the calliope hummingbird. It is only 3 inches (8 cm) long. The ruby-throated hummingbird is the only species that breeds east of the Mississippi. All the others are found in the West and Southwest. Among other species found in North America are the black-chinned, blue-throated, rufous, broad-billed, and broad-tailed hummingbirds.

HURON, Lake *See* Great Lakes

HURONS

The Huron INDIANS lived in New York State and Ontario, Canada. The Hurons were related to the IROQUOIS. They were farmers, growing corn, beans, and other crops. The Hurons were very active in the French fur trade. Quebec City is founded on the site of an old Huron trading post. In the mid-1600s, the Iroquois waged war against the Hurons. By the mid-1700s, the Hurons had fled to Ohio. In 1867 they were forced to move again, to Indian Territory in Oklahoma. The few hundred who still live there are called Wyandot.

The name "hurricane" comes from a West Indian word, *huracán*, which means "evil spirit of the sea."

HURRICANE

A hurricane is a powerful storm. Near the storm's center, or eye, the winds are 74 miles per hour (119 km/hr) or more. Some hurricanes have winds of 150

▶ *Hurricane Hugo swept its way across the Caribbean region toward South Carolina in September 1989.*

miles per hour (241 km/hr). The storm takes shape in the tropics over the ocean and builds in strength. It is circular in shape and can be between 300 and 500 miles (500 and 800 km) across. Hurricanes generally occur from June to October. In the United States, they affect the states along the Atlantic coast, especially in the South, and on the Gulf of Mexico. In the past century there have been over 500 hurricanes. Hurricanes were once given female names, but now male and female names alternate. Hurricanes can cause enormous damage. In 1979, Hurricane Frederic caused $2.3 billion in damage in the United States.

HYDROELECTRIC POWER

Hydroelectric power is electricity that is produced by the energy of falling water. Some natural waterfalls are used for this purpose. But most hydroelectric power plants are parts of DAMS. The water is stored in the dam's reservoir. It is used to turn turbines, which in turn run generators that produce electricity.

Hydroelectric power supplies less than 5 percent of the energy produced in the United States. Most energy is produced in thermal plants—those plants that use coal, natural gas, oil, and nuclear power to produce electricity. These types of plants cause pollution; hydroelectric plants do not. But the artificial lakes formed by dams destroy the habitats of plants and animals.

The Grand Coulee Dam, on the Columbia River in Washington State, is the largest hydroelectric plant in the United States.

Some Recent Hurricanes
1989 "Hugo" kills 51 in the Caribbean and the southeastern United States
1983 "Alicia" kills 21 and causes $2 billion damage in Texas
1979 "David" hits Puerto Rico and the southeastern United States: 2,000 dead
1970 "Celia" causes 11 deaths and $500 million damage in Texas
1955 "Diane" kills 184 between North Carolina and New England

Largest Hydroelectric Plants in North America
Grand Coulee (Washington State)
La Grande 2 (Canada)
Churchill Falls (Canada)
Brumley Gap (Virginia)
John Day (Oregon/Washington)
Revelstoke (Canada)
La Grande 4 (Canada)
Mica (Canada)
Bennett W.A.C. (Canada)
La Grande 3 (Canada)

◀ The Shasta Dam in central California supplies the city of Los Angeles with electricity. It is the highest overflow dam in the world: its waterfall is 480 feet (146 m) high.

ICE HOCKEY

Ice hockey is one of the most popular WINTER SPORTS in the northern United States. It is also the national sport of Canada. Many people play on frozen lakes and ponds, but organized teams usually play on indoor rinks. It is played between two teams of six players each. Goals are scored when the hard rubber disk, called the *puck*, is shot into the other team's goal. The goal is 6 feet (1.8 m) wide and 4 feet (1.2 m) high. Skillful skating makes ice hockey one of the world's fastest team sports.

Professional hockey teams throughout Canada and the United States belong to the National Hockey League. The league is divided into two conferences, which are like the two leagues in baseball. Each conference is then divided into two divisions, each with five or six teams. End-of-season play-offs each May decide which team wins the Stanley Cup and becomes the champion. Famous hockey players of the past include

▶ Ice hockey goalies wear masks to protect them against the hard rubber pucks, which travel more than 100 miles per hour (160 km/hr).

Stanley Cup Winners (NHL Champions)	
1991	Pittsburgh Penguins
1990	Edmonton Oilers
1989	Calgary Flames
1988	Edmonton Oilers
1987	Edmonton Oilers
1986	Montreal Canadiens
1985	Edmonton Oilers
1984	Edmonton Oilers
1983	New York Islanders
1982	New York Islanders
1981	New York Islanders
1980	New York Islanders
1979	Montreal Canadiens

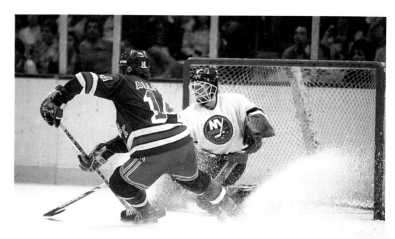

▶ Lines divide an ice hockey rink into three zones. Play starts in one of the five face-off circles. Most rinks are 200 feet (61 m) long and 85 feet (25.9 m) wide.

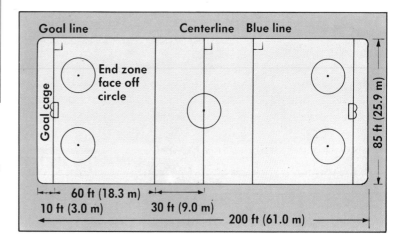

Guy Lafleur, Bobby Orr, Gordie Howe, and Ken Dryden. Top players today include Mario Lemieux, Ray Bourque, and Wayne Gretzky, who led the Edmonton Oilers to four Stanley Cups in the 1980s.

◀ *Ice-skating is a popular recreational sport. Both New Yorkers and tourists enjoy the rink at Rockefeller Center in New York City.*

Eric Heiden of the United States made Olympic history in 1980 by winning all of the men's speed skating gold medals. He took first place in five finals — 500 m, 1,000 m, 1,500 m, 5,000 m, and 10,000 m.

▼ *Speed skater Leslie Bader represented the United States in the 5,000-meter event at the 1987 World Cup.*

ICE-SKATING

Ice-skating is a popular recreational and competitive sport. There are two basic kinds, figure skating and speed skating.

Figure skating is the artistic form. It includes singles, pairs, and ice dance. Ice dance is a cross between skating and ballroom dancing. Figure skating is a popular spectator sport. Many figure skating champions go on to skate professionally in touring groups.

Speed skating involves racing on ice-covered tracks using skates with very long blades. The most popular type in North America is pack, or American-style, skating, in which a number of skaters race at once. Internationally, the most popular is Olympic-style speed skating. In this event, two skaters race each other on a two-lane track. A third type is short-track skating, in which skaters must use the skills of a sprinter.

North American and world figure skating and speed skating championships are held every year. Figure skating and speed skating events are also held at the Winter Olympic Games.

IDAHO

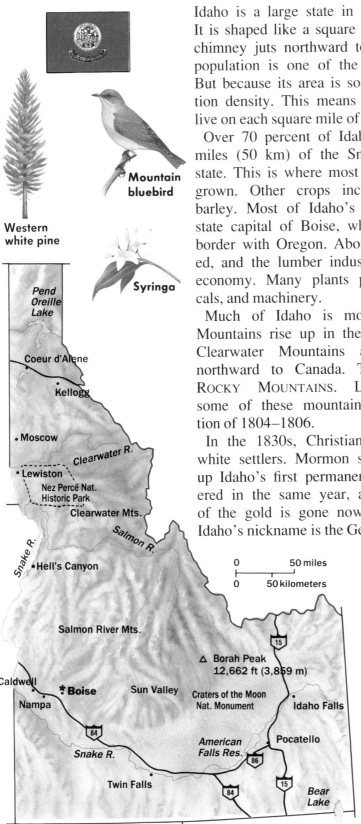

Western
white pine

Mountain
bluebird

Syringa

Pend
Oreille
Lake

Coeur d'Alene

Kellogg

Moscow

Clearwater R.

Lewiston

Nez Percé Nat.
Historic Park

Clearwater Mts.

Salmon R.

Snake R.

Hell's Canyon

Salmon River Mts.

Borah Peak
12,662 ft (3,859 m)

Caldwell

Boise

Sun Valley

Craters of the Moon
Nat. Monument

Idaho Falls

Nampa

Pocatello

Snake R.

American
Falls Res.

Twin Falls

Bear
Lake

0   50 miles

0   50 kilometers

Idaho is a large state in the northwestern United States. It is shaped like a square house with a tall chimney. This chimney juts northward to the Canadian border. Idaho's population is one of the smallest of the United States. But because its area is so large, Idaho has a low population density. This means that a small number of people live on each square mile of land in Idaho.

Over 70 percent of Idaho's population lives within 30 miles (50 km) of the Snake River in the south of the state. This is where most of Idaho's famous potatoes are grown. Other crops include wheat, sugar beets, and barley. Most of Idaho's crops are shipped through the state capital of Boise, which is near the state's western border with Oregon. About two fifths of Idaho is forested, and the lumber industry is an important part of the economy. Many plants produce food products, chemicals, and machinery.

Much of Idaho is mountainous. The Salmon River Mountains rise up in the western part of the state. The Clearwater Mountains and Bitterroot Range extend northward to Canada. These ranges are part of the ROCKY MOUNTAINS. LEWIS AND CLARK explored some of these mountains during their famous expedition of 1804–1806.

In the 1830s, Christian missionaries became the first white settlers. Mormon settlers arrived in 1860 and set up Idaho's first permanent settlement. Gold was discovered in the same year, and more settlers arrived. Most of the gold is gone now, but mining is still important. Idaho's nickname is the Gem State.

Idaho

Capital: Boise
Area: 82,412 sq mi (213,447 km²). Rank: 13th
Population: 1,011,986 (1990). Rank: 42nd
Statehood: July 3, 1890
Principal rivers: Snake, Salmon, Clearwater, Kootenai
Highest point: Borah Peak, 12,662 ft (3,859 m)
Motto: *Esto Perpetua* (May It Endure Forever)
Song: "Here We Have Idaho"

▲ The submerged rocks in Hell's Canyon National Recreation Area are covered with silt carried by the Snake River.

► Cattle farmers collect hay for the winter. Idaho produces nearly 5 million tons of hay each year.

▼ Silver City Ghost Town is a relic of Idaho's mining boom in the mid-1800s.

Places of Interest
● Hell's Canyon, on the Snake River, has an average depth of about 1 mi (1.6 km).
● Nez Percé National Historical Park, near Lewiston, honors the Nez Percé Indians and the Lewis and Clark Expedition.
● Sun Valley, in southern Idaho, is one of the country's most famous ski resorts.

ILLINOIS

ILLINOIS

Cardinal

White oak

Illinois native violet

Illinois is a leading farming and industrial state. It is located in the Midwest. Its largest city, CHICAGO, is a major port on Lake Michigan. The state's western border is the Mississippi River, so goods can be sent easily and cheaply from Illinois. Much of the land of Illinois is flat and fertile, and one of its nicknames is the Prairie State. Large quantities of corn, soybeans, wheat, oats, barley, rye, and sorghum are grown in Illinois. Cattle farming is also practiced on a large scale. There are more than 2.5 million cattle in Illinois.

Many different types of goods are produced by Illinois factories. Manufactured goods account for more than ten times the income provided by farming. The state's major products include machinery, petroleum products, electronic equipment, and chemicals. Mining is an important industry in the southern part of the

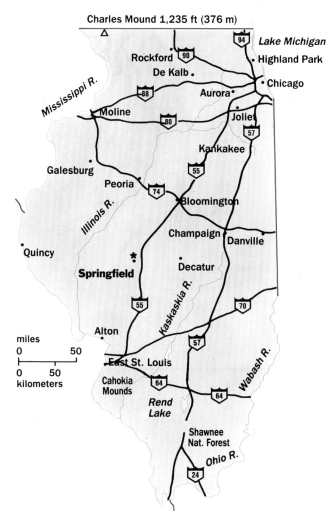

Places of Interest
- Abraham Lincoln's home, in Springfield, has been preserved as a national historic site.
- Monk's Mound, one of the Cahokia Mounds, is the largest Indian mound in the country.
- Chicago has all the cultural and sporting attractions expected of one of the world's great cities.
- Shawnee National Forest stretches across nine counties of southern Illinois.

state. The factories and stockyards of Illinois were also important for the labor movement in the United States. Many of the modern labor unions were formed in the 1800s or early 1900s in Illinois.

The name "Illinois" comes from the Indians who lived in the area long ago. They called themselves *Illinewek*, or "superior men." The first white settlers were French fur traders in the early 1600s. After the FRENCH AND INDIAN WAR, Great Britain gained control of the region. Illinois grew in population and importance because of its location and good farmland. After the opening of the ERIE CANAL, Illinois attracted many settlers from the east. Abraham LINCOLN grew up in Illinois, and the state is known as the Land of Lincoln.

▲ The 110-story Sears Building in Chicago is the world's tallest skyscraper.

◄ Many goods from Illinois are shipped from Lake Michigan. A series of drawbridges lets ships enter downtown Chicago.

Illinois
Capital: Springfield
Area: 55,645 sq mi (144,120 km²). Rank: 24th
Population: 11,466,682 (1990). Rank: 6th
Principal rivers: Mississippi, Ohio, Illinois, Wabash
Highest point: Charles Mound, 1,235 ft (376 m)
Motto: State Sovereignty, National Union
Song: "Illinois"

◄ Illinois farmers harvest more than 1 billion bushels of corn each year. Only Iowa produces more.

▶ *Many long or difficult names were changed by 19th-century immigration officials at Ellis Island, New York.*

Immigration Facts
● Of the 250 million Americans, almost 140 million trace their ancestry to the United Kingdom, Germany, and Ireland.
● In recent years, some 500,000 to 600,000 immigrants have entered the United States annually.
● From 1901 to 1910, the United States received 8.8 million immigrants—more than in any other decade.

Immigrants to the U.S. in 1987 by Place of Birth	
Asia:	257,700
Caribbean:	102,900
Central America and Mexico:	101,700
Europe:	61,200
South America:	44,400
Africa:	17,700
Canada:	11,900
Other countries:	2,000
Australia and New Zealand:	1,900

IMMIGRATION

Immigration takes place when people come to live in a country from another one. Because more immigrants have come to the United States than any other country, it is known as a "nation of immigrants." Between 1820 and 1987, more than 53 million immigrants entered the United States legally. Most of them eventually obtained U.S. CITIZENSHIP through a process called naturalization. Millions more have come as illegal immigrants— without papers giving them the right to stay permanently. A law passed in 1986 makes it easier for them to stay in the United States and become citizens.

Before World War I, almost anyone could enter the United States legally. A series of laws then made immigration more difficult. Most immigrants landed at Ellis Island in New York Harbor, where they were investigated by agents of the U.S. Immigration and Naturalization Service. Between 1920 and 1965, immigration was restricted in such a way that people from northern and western Europe had the best chance of entering. Now people with skills that are needed and relatives of U.S. citizens are admitted first, regardless of what country they come from.

In a sense, the American Indians were the first American immigrants. They migrated to the Americas from Asia in the far-distant past. Every other American either was born in another country or descends from people who came from another country. Before 1965, most immigrants came from Europe. Since then, most have come from Latin America and Asia.

IMPEACHMENT

Impeachment is a process that is followed when a government official is accused of a crime or abuse of his or her office. Legally, an impeachment is an accusation. But the term is also used for the trial. In the United States, at the federal level, only the House of Representatives can impeach an official. The Senate then tries the impeached official; a two-thirds vote is necessary for conviction. Impeachment is rarely used. The most famous impeachment was that of President Andrew JOHNSON in 1868. He was found to be not guilty—by one vote. In 1974, President Richard NIXON resigned when it became clear that he was to be impeached.

In the history of the United States, the Senate has sat on only eleven impeachment trials. Only four of the accused, all federal judges, were convicted. Conviction in an impeachment results in the person being removed from office and disqualified to hold "any office of honor, trust, or profit under the United States."

INDEPENDENCE DAY

Independence Day, July 4, is the birthday of the United States. That was the day, in 1776, when the CONTINENTAL CONGRESS adopted the DECLARATION OF INDEPENDENCE. The first celebration of Independence Day was in Philadelphia, on July 8, 1776, when the Declaration of Independence was first read to the public. The LIBERTY BELL rang out from the tower of the State House (now INDEPENDENCE HALL). From then on, the idea of celebrating Independence Day spread throughout the growing country. Independence Day has been a legal federal holiday since 1941.

 On July 8, 1776, the Liberty Bell proclaimed the news of the Declaration of Independence from the tower of Independence Hall in Philadelphia.

INDEPENDENCE HALL

Independence Hall, in PHILADELPHIA, is considered the birthplace of the United States. Delegates to the Second CONTINENTAL CONGRESS met there in 1775 and appointed George WASHINGTON commander in chief of the Continental Army. The following year the delegates met there again to declare the American colonies independent and sign the DECLARATION OF INDEPENDENCE. On July 8, 1776, the LIBERTY BELL, then in the hall's tower, rang out to proclaim the news. The ARTICLES OF CONFEDERATION were adopted in Independence Hall in 1781, and six years later the U.S. CONSTITUTION was drafted there.

Independence Hall was built in 1732 and originally served as the Pennsylvania State House. Today it is part of the Independence National Historical Park.

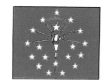

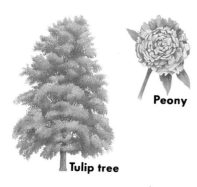

Tulip tree

Peony

Cardinal

Indiana is an important farming and industrial state in the Midwest. In the northwest, it borders Lake Michigan. The Ohio River forms the state's southern boundary. Indiana has rich farmlands. Corn is the chief crop, but soybeans and wheat are also grown on Indiana farms. Over 4 million hogs and pigs and 1.5 million head of cattle are raised in Indiana. Nearly 95 percent of Indiana's farm goods are sent to other parts of the country.

Industry is even more important than agriculture for Indiana. Industrial income first passed farming income early in the 1900s. Coal mines and limestone quarries were among the first industrial ventures in Indiana. Then oil refineries, steel mills, and factories were built in the northern Indiana cities of Gary, Fort Wayne, and South Bend. The Lake Michigan lakefront became a major industrial region. The factories there provided many people with jobs. But they also caused pollution. New laws have begun to control much of the dangerous pollution and preserve wild areas on the Lake Michigan shoreline. Visitors can now relax in the dunes and forests of the Indiana Dunes National Lakeshore.

Indiana got its name because so many Indian tribes once lived there. Some fierce battles between the U.S. Army and Indian tribes took place in Indiana. The last battle was in 1811. General William Henry HARRISON defeated the Miami Indians in the Battle of Tippecanoe. This cleared the way for permanent white settlements. The victory at Tippecanoe later helped Harrison become U.S. president.

Indiana
Capital: Indianapolis
Area: 35,932 sq mi (93,064 km²). Rank: 38th
Population: 5,564,228 (1990). Rank: 14th
Statehood: Dec. 11, 1816
Principal rivers: Ohio, Wabash, White, Tippecanoe
Highest point: Wayne County, near Richmond, 1,257 ft (383 m)
Motto: The Crossroads of America
Song: "On the Banks of the Wabash, Far Away"

► *The well-managed farms of Steuben County, near the borders with Michigan and Ohio, produce hogs, poultry, and vegetables.*

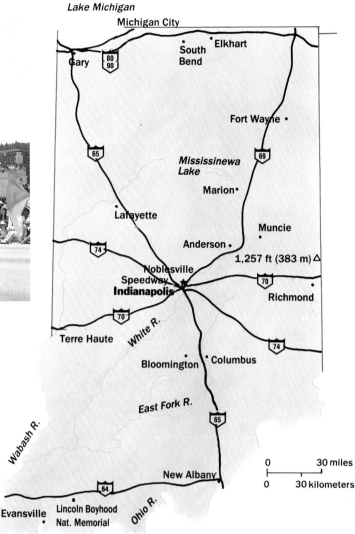

▲ Memorial Day parades held in Indianapolis also celebrate the Indianapolis 500, one of the world's greatest and most popular automobile races.

▼ Lake Tippecanoe is located in the northern part of Indiana, between South Bend and Fort Wayne. Dozens of lakes around the state offer good swimming, boating, and fishing.

Places of Interest
● The Indianapolis Motor Speedway, in Speedway, is the home of the Indianapolis 500 automobile race.
● Historic Fort Wayne, a reconstructed fortress, stands on the site of an American Army fort of 1816.
● Conner Prairie Settlement, in Noblesville, is a glimpse into the Indian way of life of the early 1800s.

▲ *Indiana's state capitol, built in 1878, is located in the heart of Indianapolis.*

INDIANAPOLIS

Indianapolis is the capital and largest city of INDIANA, with a population of 741,952. It is at the geographic heart of the state. It is an important transportation center for the surrounding farming area. Most goods passing between Ohio and Illinois go through Indianapolis. Meat packing is also important. Stockyards cover more than 210 acres (85 ha). Indianapolis is the Midwest regional center for many insurance companies. It is the home of Indiana University and a campus of Purdue University. College football, professional basketball, and the famous Indianapolis 500 automobile race are top sports attractions.

INDIANS, American

American Indians are the native peoples of the Western Hemisphere. They have been living in the Americas for many thousands of years. When Christopher Columbus arrived in America, he thought he was in the East Indies and called the people he met "Indians." At that time there were between 1 million and 6 million Indians in what is now the United States and Canada. They had come to America from Asia by crossing from Siberia to Alaska and then moving south. This migration started about 30,000 years ago.

Many of the Indians in North America north of Mexico lived by hunting and fishing, growing maize (corn), and gathering nuts, berries, and wild grains. Those who lived east of the Mississippi River included

▼ *A Navajo Ganado rug usually has a deep red background and gold designs.*

Navajo blanket

▶ *Woven "elbow baskets" were a specialty of the Choctaw, Chickasaw, and Creek tribes.*

Southeast elbow basket

▼ *Cheyenne babies were put in finely stitched cradle boards.*

Cheyenne cradle board

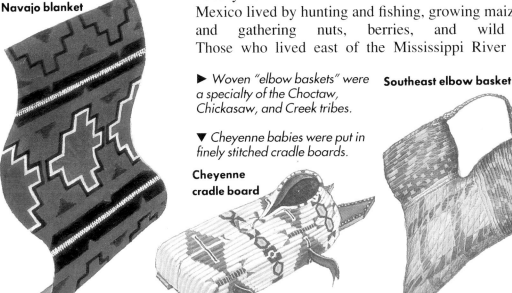

Eastern Woodlands moccasins

Plains pipe

◀ *Eastern moccasins were made of a single piece of leather. Plains Indians often decorated their pipes with colorful patterned weavings.*

▼ *Traditional Indian houses suit the climate and terrain of various tribes.*

Plains tepee

Major Regions of Indian Tribes and Culture
Eastern Woodland: the forests and fields of the East.
Plains: the open plains — home of the buffalo.
Plateau: along the Columbia River of the Pacific Northwest.
Great Basin: the desert regions between the Rockies and the Sierra Nevadas of eastern California.
Southwest: the dry highlands of Arizona and New Mexico.
Northwest Coast: the fishing area of the northern Pacific coast of Oregon and Washington.
California: mountains, forest, rich farmland, and desert.

Paiute brush wickiup

Northwest Coast plank house

◀ *Frederic Remington's painting of a Cheyenne brave shows how naturally the Plains Indians took to horseback riding.*

345

▶ *The Apache warrior Geronimo, seen here behind the wheel of an early Ford automobile, was a cattle rancher in his last years.*

Many Indian place-names are clues about local geography: Connecticut ("long river place"); Massachusetts ("large hill place"); Michigan ("great water"); Mississippi ("great river"); Missouri ("muddy water"); Ohio ("fine or good river"); and Wisconsin ("grassy place").

▼ *Indians occupied all of North America before the arrival of Europeans. Each tribe was composed of many smaller tribes sharing the language and customs.*

Algonquian-speaking peoples, the IROQUOIS League, or Confederacy, and what became known as the Five Civilized tribes of the Southeast. The Indians of the Great Plains, with their tepees and feathered head-dresses, are the Indians most often seen in movies. Among these people were the Sioux. They hunted the bison (buffalo), riding horses after they were brought to the New World by Europeans.

The Indians of the Northwest became famous for their totem poles and other wood carvings. The Pueblo Indians of the Southwest were farmers noted for their woven baskets and pottery.

Aleut

Cree

Cree

Chippewa

Blackfoot

Algonquin

Territories

- ☐ Arctic
- ☐ Subarctic
- ▨ Northwest Coast
- ☐ California
- ☐ Plains
- ☐ Eastern Woodlands
- ▨ Southwest

Chinook

Crow

Mandan

Nez Percé
Shoshoni

Sioux

Cheyenne

Huron Mohawk

Iroquois

Pawnee

Miami Mohican

Paiute

Ute

Arapaho

Powhatan

Kiowa

Cherokee

Navajo
Hopi Pueblo

Comanche

Creek

Caddo

Apache

Choctaw

Seminole

◀ *Kwakiutl craftsmen of the Pacific Northwest continue the tradition of carving totem poles from cedar logs.*

Many Indian tribes in the East lost their lands to white settlers. In the West, however, many were put on reservations. There are now about 1.5 million Indians in the United States. About one third of them live on reservations. Almost 500,000 Indians live in Canada. The states with the largest numbers of Indians are Oklahoma, Arizona, New Mexico, North Carolina, and California. One half of the total Indian population lives in these five states. The Navajos form the largest Indian

▲ *Young Indians learned crafts and skills such as weaving and hunting. But they still had time for games and sports.*

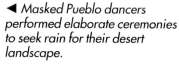

◀ *Masked Pueblo dancers performed elaborate ceremonies to seek rain for their desert landscape.*

▲ *This Navajo ranger at Grand Canyon National Park can teach visitors about her tribe's long history in the area.*

Indian Loss of Lands: Some Important Dates

1768: Colonial treaties with Iroquois, Creeks, and Cherokees give settlers more land.

1795: United States gains territory in Ohio from Delaware, Shawnee, Wyandot, and Miami tribes.

1818: Chickasaws sell all their land above Tennessee's southern border.

1825: Georgia gains large areas from Creeks; Osage and Kansas tribes give up land in Missouri Territory.

1828: Arkansas Territory gains Cherokee land.

1832: Sauk (or Sac) Indians give up lands east of Mississippi River.

1851: Sioux sign away lands in Iowa and Minnesota.

1863: Congress removes all Indians from Kansas.

1885: Ahantchuyuks give up land in Oregon.

nation. Their reservation covers all the northeastern corner of Arizona and extends into Utah and New Mexico. Many Sioux live in South Dakota and Oklahoma and Cherokees in North Carolina.

The Indians have been wards of the U.S. government since 1871. Their affairs have been managed by the Bureau of Indian Affairs, a division of the U.S. Department of the Interior. In the 1970s, the Indians began to make strong demands to manage their own affairs. And they began fighting to have their lands returned to them or to get financial settlement. In many cases, their lands had been taken away from them in violation of treaties.

Poverty is widespread among Indians. Their unemployment rate far exceeds that of the general population. Fewer than 50 percent graduate from high school. And their birth, death, and suicide rates are probably the highest in the nation. But with the return of some of their lands, it is hoped that many Indians will be able to achieve a better way of life. The Bureau of Indian Affairs is trying hard to accomplish this. Its staff is now two-thirds Indian, and they are providing better educational opportunities, as well as job training.

This encyclopedia contains articles on many Indian tribes and their great leaders. You may want to look them up in the Index.

INDIAN WARS

When the Europeans discovered the New World, they claimed the land and all its riches. When white settlers moved onto the lands occupied by Native Americans, war became inevitable. In what is now the United States, these wars began in the early 1600s in Virginia and New England. When France and England fought for control of North America in the 1700s, most Indian tribes supported the losing side, the French. During the American REVOLUTION, most tribes again backed the losing side, the British.

After the WAR OF 1812, the Indians had no European allies to help them. The Black Hawk War (1831–1832) ended with the Sauk and Fox expelled from the upper Mississippi Valley. Most of the Seminoles of Florida were defeated by 1842 and moved west of the Mississippi River. There, also, the Indians had their lands taken by white settlers. Tribes like the

Apaches and the Sioux resisted. The Sioux defeated U.S. troops under General George A. CUSTER at the Battle of the Little Bighorn in 1876. The last battle between U.S. troops and Indians was at Wounded Knee, South Dakota, in 1890, where Sioux men, women, and children were massacred.

▲ *Fierce battles between Indian warriors and the U.S. Army were common in the 1800s. The Indians were outnumbered and defeated by modern weapons.*

INDUSTRIAL REVOLUTION

Industrial Revolution is the name given to the change from an economy based mostly on growing crops and raising livestock to one based on turning out large amounts of manufactured goods.

The Industrial Revolution first took place in England. It started in the mid-1700s. James Watt's steam engine freed factories from depending on waterpower. Improvements in iron making made it possible to make good, durable machines and parts. With the growth of factories, the nature of work also changed. People had to perform the same tasks over and over again with little or no rest.

Even before independence, Americans were making iron, ships, and small arms. Eli WHITNEY's invention of the cotton gin in 1793 and Robert FULTON's first steamboat in 1807 were important steps in the U.S. Industrial Revolution. The first big factories were mostly textile mills in New England that still depended on water for power. By 1850, however, the United States was on the way to becoming the greatest manufacturing nation in the world.

▼ *The Industrial Revolution in the United States initially centered around textile mills in New England. This woodcut shows a woman spinning yarn.*

INSECTS

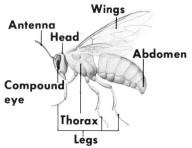

▼ An insect has three body sections, the head, thorax, and abdomen. Inside the abdomen are the stomach, reproductive organs, and breathing tubes.

Wings
Antenna
Head
Abdomen
Compound eye
Thorax
Legs

An insect is a small animal with six legs and a body divided into three parts. Insects are found everywhere, from deserts to glaciers, from hot springs to cold waterfalls. Scientists know of more than 800,000 species, or kinds, of insects in the world. About 80,000 of these are found in North America. One of the largest is the cecropia moth, of eastern North America. It has a wingspan of up to 6 inches (15 cm). The smallest is a type of fairy fly found on the Pacific coast. It is less than 1/100th of an inch (0.5 mm) long.

Insects are divided into major groups, or orders. The orders that include the most species are the BEETLES, BUTTERFLIES AND MOTHS, ANTS, BEES and wasps, and true flies. In one square yard of soil, up to 2,000 insects can be found. Most of these are less than 1/4 inch (6 mm) long.

Insects are important in the balance of nature. A few, such as honeybees, also provide products people need. Only a few hundred species of North American insects are harmful. But these insects destroy about a tenth of the crops grown in a

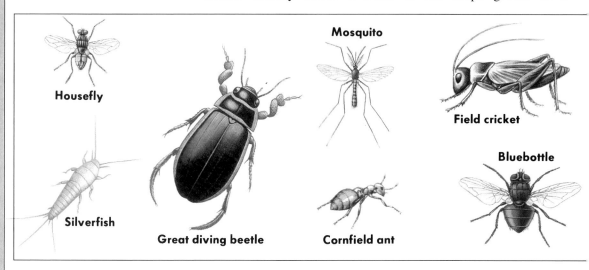

Housefly

Mosquito

Field cricket

Silverfish

Great diving beetle

Cornfield ant

Bluebottle

Because insects are cold-blooded, their pulse rate may range from 140 per minute in an active insect to 1 pulse per *hour* in chilled insects. Insects may vibrate their wings at speeds up to 1,000 beats per second, which is about 12 times faster than the wing beat of the hummingbird.

year. This damage, along with various methods of preventing it, costs the United States billions of dollars every year. Serious pests include the boll weevil, which feeds on cotton, and the Colorado potato beetle, which feeds on potatoes. The Japanese beetle attacks plants in farms, orchards, and gardens. The Hessian fly, corn earworm, flour beetle, and chinch bug destroy grain crops.

Some insects are household pests. These include the silverfish, clothes moth, carpet beetle, ant, and termite. A few insects, such as the human louse, some mosquitoes, and the common housefly, carry disease. Still others, like the "no-see-'em" (a type of midge) of New England, give unpleasant bites. Insecticides (chemicals that kill insects) are one method of controlling insect pests, but many farmers prefer using natural methods, such as using other insects to eat pests.

We now know that many of the chemicals once used to kill insect pests have serious side effects on humans. Safer, "natural" methods have become common. For example, the insect-eating mosquitofish has been introduced to many farming districts.

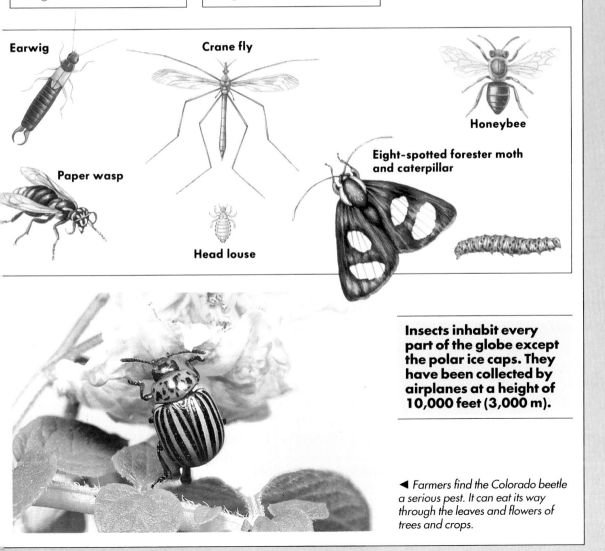

Earwig

Crane fly

Honeybee

Paper wasp

Eight-spotted forester moth and caterpillar

Head louse

Insects inhabit every part of the globe except the polar ice caps. They have been collected by airplanes at a height of 10,000 feet (3,000 m).

◀ *Farmers find the Colorado beetle a serious pest. It can eat its way through the leaves and flowers of trees and crops.*

▼ *The safety razor and sewing machine were invented in 19th-century America.*

Safety razor

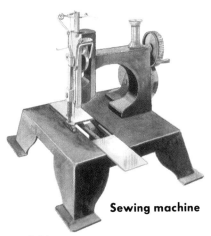

Sewing machine

INSURANCE INDUSTRY

Insurance exists to provide people with protection against unforeseen events. People pay a certain sum (called a premium) to insurers. In return the insurer assumes the risk of paying compensation for the loss of life or damage to health or property. Life insurance provides payments to the next of kin in the event of the policyholder's death. In the United States, the average family has about $70,000 in life insurance. Health insurance pays doctor and hospital bills and other medical expenses. The most important kinds of property insurance are auto and home-owners insurance.

There are private insurers and government insurers. Among the latter is the federal government, which provides health insurance for the elderly through Medicare. More than 2 million people work in the U.S. insurance industry.

INTERIOR, Department of the *See* Government, U.S.

INVENTIONS

An invention is something that has been made for the first time. Americans have invented many useful things, from the safety pin, zipper, and sewing machine to the airplane, nuclear reactor, and laser. Following is a list of some of the most important American inventors and their inventions.

Famous American Inventions and Inventors		
Invention	Inventor	Date
Air brake	George Westinghouse	1869
Air conditioning	Willis H. Carrier	1902
Airplane	Orville and Wilbur Wright	1903
Bakelite (plastic)	Leo Baekeland	1907
CAT scanner	Allan Cormack	1968
Computer, electronic digital	J. Presper Eckert, Jr., and John W. Mauchly	1946
Cotton gin	Eli Whitney	1793
Cyclotron	Ernest O. Lawrence	1931
Electromagnet	Joseph Henry	1828
Electronic flash	Harold E. Edgerton	1931
Elevator	Elisha G. Otis	1853
Escalator	Jesse Reno	1892
Gyrocompass	Elmer Sperry	1911
Helicopter	Igor Sikorsky	1939

Incandescent lamp	Thomas Alva Edison	1879
Laser	Theodore Maiman	1960
Lightning rod	Benjamin Franklin	1752
Lock, pin-tumble	Linus Yale, Jr.	1865
Locomotive (first U.S.)	Peter Cooper	1830
Machine gun	Richard Gatling	1861
Motion-picture projector	Thomas Alva Edison	1888
Motor, AC	Nikola Tesla	1887
Nuclear reactor	Enrico Fermi and others	1942
Nylon	Wallace H. Carothers	1936
Pen, fountain	Lewis E. Waterman	1884
Pen, ball-point	John Loud	1888
Phonograph	Thomas Alva Edison	1877
Polaroid camera	Edwin H. Land	1947
Reaper	Cyrus McCormack	1834
Revolver	Samuel Colt	1835
Rocket, liquid-fuel	Robert Goddard	1926
Safety pin	Walter Hunt	1849
Sewing machine	Elias Howe	1846
Sleeping car (train)	George Pullman	1865
Steamboat	Robert Fulton	1807
Submarine, power-driven	John. P. Holland	1887
Telegraph	Samuel F.B. Morse	1837
Telephone	Alexander Graham Bell	1876
Television	Vladimir Zworykin	1923
Transistor	John Bardeen, Walter Brattain, William Shockley	1948
Trolley car, electric	Frank Sprague	1887
Typewriter	Christopher L. Sholes, Carlos S. Glidden, and Samuel W. Soule	1868
Videotape recorder	Charles Ginsberg and Charles Anderson	1956
Vulcanization of rubber	Charles S. Goodyear	1839
Xerography (photocopying)	Chester Carlson	1942
X-ray tube	William D. Coolidge	1913
Zipper	W.L. Judson	1896

One day in 1849, New York inventor William Hunt was twisting wire while thinking of a way to repay a $15 debt. After three hours he had designed the modern safety pin, which he patented that year.

There is always a need for new inventions. One 1990 invention was a "garbage collector" for space vehicles. This device can prevent spacecraft from colliding with other orbiting material.

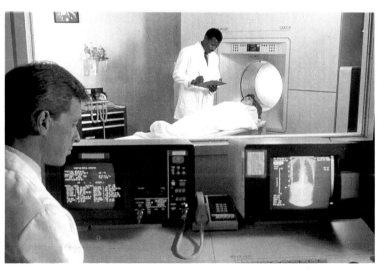

◄ *CAT scanners use X rays to provide doctors with a picture "slice" of a patient's body. Allan Cormack of the United States and Geoffrey Hounsfield of the United Kingdom shared the 1979 Nobel Prize for medicine, awarded for their work in developing the CAT scanner.*

IOWA

Wild rose

Eastern goldfinch

Oak

When people think of the Midwest state of Iowa, they usually think of fields of corn, tassels swaying in the breeze. The Hawkeye State, as it is called, is known for rich farmland. It usually ranks first (or second to Illinois) among states each year in the amount of corn grown. Feeding on the corn, and also on soybeans, are

▶ *The mighty Mississippi River forms Iowa's eastern border and irrigates its fertile farms.*

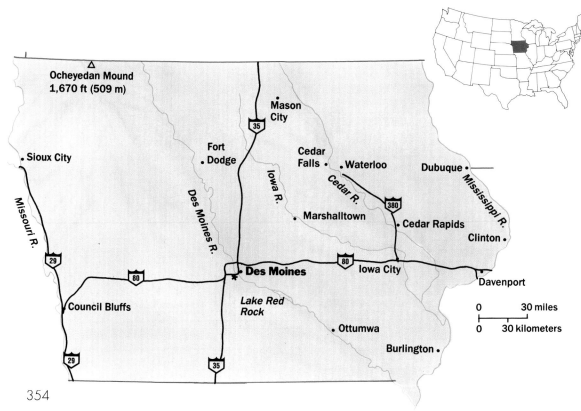

large numbers of hogs and cattle. Iowa raises more hogs and pigs than any other state. Once the crops and livestock leave the farms, Iowa factories turn them into meat, breakfast cereals, animal feeds, and other food products. But many other goods—especially farm machinery—are made in Iowa. And Des Moines, the state capital and Iowa's biggest city, is a center of the insurance industry.

One reason Iowa is good for growing crops is that the land is flat or gently rolling. The other reason is that glaciers melted at the end of the last Ice Age and left behind fertile rock and soil. The two longest rivers in North America provide irrigation water in case of drought. The Mississippi borders Iowa on the east, and the Missouri on the west. Both allow cheap transport of bulk goods such as grain to other parts of the country.

The first Europeans to visit Iowa were the French explorers and fur trappers. In 1803 it was sold to the United States as part of the LOUISIANA PURCHASE. In 1832 an uprising by Sauk (or Sac) and Fox Indians was put down, and eastern Iowa soon filled with settlers. It became a U.S. territory in 1838 and was admitted to the Union as the 29th state in 1846.

Iowa
Capital: Des Moines
Area: 55,965 sq mi (144,950 km^2). Rank: 25th
Population: 2,787,424 (1990). Rank: 30th
Statehood: Dec. 28, 1846
Principal rivers: Missouri, Mississippi, Des Moines
Highest point: Osceola County, border with Minnesota, 1,670 ft (509 m)
Motto: Our Liberties We Prize and Our Rights We Will Maintain
Song: "The Song of Iowa"

Places of Interest
● Living History Farms, near Des Moines, is a working farm with buildings and implements from the late 1800s.
● Floyd Monument, a 100-foot (30-m) stone shaft in Sioux City, honors Charles Floyd of the Lewis and Clark Expedition.
● The Iowa State Fair, held each August in Des Moines, is one of the largest in the country.

◀ *The gilded dome of the Capitol Building in Des Moines dominates the skyline. Inside are murals and mosaics.*

IRON AND STEEL INDUSTRY

Iron and steel production is one of the world's most important industries. Between 1896 and 1970 the United States was the leading producer of iron and steel in the world. In 1971 it was overtaken by the Soviet Union. Today Japan also produces more steel than the United States. More than two thirds of U.S. steel is produced by just five states: Pennsylvania, Indiana, Ohio, Illinois, and Michigan.

Steel is made from iron ore. In the United States, most iron ore is mined in Minnesota and Michigan, near Lake Superior. California, Missouri, and Wyoming are other important sources.

The first successful ironworks in the United States was established in 1646, at Saugus, Massachusetts. The U.S. steel industry began in the late 1800s, following the discovery of the iron ore deposits near Lake Superior. In 1873, Andrew CARNEGIE built the first large steel plant in the country, in Pennsylvania. There are now about 160 steel plants in the United States, owned by about 80 private companies. The United States Steel Corporation is the largest. The automobile and construction industries are major users of steel.

The United States produces about 10 percent of the world's steel, down from 20 percent in 1970. But it imports more steel than any other country.

▼ *Molten iron is poured into a furnace before being cast into steel. First it is heated to 2,800°F (1,500°C).*

◀ Iroquois longhouse villages lined the shores of Lakes Erie and Ontario. Their strange wooden masks represented mythological beings and were worn during tribal ceremonies.

IROQUOIS LEAGUE

The Iroquois League was a federation of Indian tribes that lived in what is now northern New York State. The League was founded in the 1500s by the Cayuga, MOHAWK, Oneida, Onondaga, and Seneca Indians and was called the Iroquois League of Five Nations. When the Tuscaroras joined in the early 1700s, it became the League of Six Nations. The Iroquois were involved in trade first with the Dutch and then with the British, who took over from the Dutch. The Iroquois helped the British to win the French and Indian War in the mid-1700s. During the American Revolution, four of the six tribes fought for the British. Today the base of the Iroquois confederacy is at the Onondaga Reservation, near Syracuse, New York. However, many Iroquois live on reservations in other parts of the United States and in Canada. (See also HIAWATHA.)

IWO JIMA, Battle of

Iwo Jima is a volcanic island about 750 miles (1,450 km) south of Tokyo, Japan. It was the scene of one of the fiercest battles of WORLD WAR II. The American victory was vital for the Allies. The Japanese had used Iwo Jima as an air base throughout the war. The U.S. MARINES finally captured the island near the end of the war, on March 17, 1945. But during the month of fighting, 6,800 Marines were killed and more than 18,000 were wounded. After the war the United States governed the island. It was returned to Japan in 1968.

▼ Iwo Jima's location made it an important air base for U.S. forces on their way toward Japan. Military leaders used the term "island hopping" to describe this path to Japan.

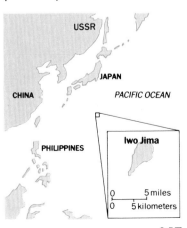

JACK-IN-THE-PULPIT

The jack-in-the-pulpit is a North American wildflower that grows in damp places. It gets its name from the way it looks. The plant's small flowers are on a stalk-like structure called a spadix. Another part of the plant, the spathe, forms a hood over the spadix. The two structures resemble a person standing in a pulpit.

The jack-in-the-pulpit is sometimes called "Indian turnip" because early white settlers saw Indians cooking the root in the same way that they cooked turnips. But it is dangerous to eat this plant because some parts are poisonous if not cooked properly.

JACKRABBIT

The jackrabbit is a large HARE that lives on the grassy plains of the western United States. Most jackrabbits eat crops and are considered pests by farmers. Like other hares, jackrabbits have long hind legs, long ears, and short tails.

Jackrabbits have brownish-gray fur. But the fur of the white-tailed jackrabbit, which lives in the Northwest, turns white during the winter. The black-tailed jackrabbit is the largest jackrabbit. It can grow up to 2 feet (60 cm) in length and weigh 9 pounds (4 kg). Because it has long, donkeylike ears, it is also known as the jackass hare. Other North American jackrabbits include the antelope, California, and white-shouldered jackrabbits.

▲ Some Indian tribes ate jack-in-the-pulpits, but only after carefully preparing them to remove poisonous crystals.

▶ The jackrabbit needs its speed (up to 35 miles per hour, or 60 km/hr) to escape from coyotes. It can jump 20 feet (6 m).

JACKSON, Andrew

Andrew Jackson was the seventh president of the United States. He was the first president to rise from humble origins. He campaigned under the slogan "Let the people rule" and founded the modern Democratic Party. A strong leader, Jackson expanded the power of the presidency.

Jackson was a frontiersman who was called "Old Hickory" because of his toughness. He was also a successful businessman and served in Congress and as a judge. As a major general in the WAR OF 1812, he defeated the Creek Indians and routed the British in the Battle of New Orleans. Jackson became a national hero. He was made governor of the Territory of Florida and was then elected senator from Tennessee. In 1828 he was elected president.

Andrew Jackson
Born: March 15, 1767, in Waxhaw Settlement, South Carolina
Education: Legal studies in law office
Political party: Democratic
Term of office: 1829–1837
Married: 1791 to Mrs. Rachel Donelson Robards
Died: June 8, 1845, in Nashville, Tennessee

◀ Jackson's troops repelled the British attack on New Orleans in 1815.

▼ Andrew Jackson was captured by the British during the Revolutionary War. An officer slashed him with a sword for refusing to polish his shoes.

Jackson said he was in favor of states' rights. As president, he supported the southern states that forcibly expelled their Indian populations in spite of federal treaties and court decisions. But he threatened to send troops to South Carolina if the state ignored or nullified an unpopular federal tariff law.

Jackson's biggest battle was against the Bank of the United States. This bank dominated banking in the country, and Jackson felt that it was unfair to the West. He crippled the bank by withdrawing federal funds and placing them in state banks. Many of these banks were unsound, however. A financial panic in 1837 caused great damage to the national economy.

In 1837, after serving two terms as president, Jackson retired to his home, the Hermitage, in Tennessee.

JACKSON, Jesse

The Reverend Jesse Jackson (1941–   ) is a political and CIVIL RIGHTS leader. He was born in Greenville, South Carolina. Jackson, a Baptist minister, took part in the civil rights protests in the South with Martin Luther KING, Jr., in the 1960s. He founded PUSH (People United to Save Humanity) in 1971. Its aim was to increase economic opportunities for blacks. Jackson also encouraged black youths to get a good education. In 1984 and 1988, he sought the Democratic nomination for president. He did not succeed. But by the time of the 1988 campaign, he had many followers and was in a position to influence Democratic policy at the nominating convention.

▲ Jesse Jackson's hard work on behalf of the poor led to his having a strong voice in national politics. His missions to Syria and Cuba helped secure the release of American prisoners.

JACKSON, Mahalia

Mahalia Jackson (1911–1972) was the most famous gospel singer in the world. She was born in New Orleans and began singing in the choir of the church where her father preached. She moved to Chicago when she was 17, taking jobs in factories and as a hotel chambermaid. In her free time she continued singing in a local Baptist church. Jackson's strong voice and spirited style attracted many admirers. She began making records in the 1930s and continued until her death 40 years later.

▼ Stonewall Jackson's brilliant victory at Bull Run silenced any Northerners who thought the war would be over in days. His death in 1863 was a severe loss for the Confederate cause, and in particular for General Lee, who called Jackson "my right arm."

JACKSON, Thomas Jonathan "Stonewall"

Thomas "Stonewall" Jackson (1824–1863) was a brilliant Confederate general. He was born in Clarksburg, Virginia (now West Virginia). He attended West Point and fought with distinction in the MEXICAN WAR (1846–1848). Later, he taught at the Virginia Military Institute. There his serious nature made him somewhat unpopular with cadets. But later, as a combat officer, he won the respect and love of his troops.

After the start of the CIVIL WAR, Jackson was made a brigadier general in the Confederate Army. He acquired the nickname "Stonewall" at the first BATTLE OF BULL RUN in July 1861. Jackson held his troops in a strong line, resisting heavy enemy fire. "There is Jackson standing like a stone wall!" cried another officer to his own retreating troops. "Let us determine to die here and we will conquer!"

Later, in such important ..tles as Fredericksburg (1862) and Chancellorsville (1863), Jackson's cool head and mastery of surprise tactics helped to achieve Southern victories. At Chancellorsville he was accidentally shot by his own men.

JACKSONVILLE

Jacksonville is FLORIDA's largest city, with a population of 672,971. It is located on the St. Johns River in the northeastern corner of the state. Jacksonville was founded in 1822 when Florida became a U.S. territory. It is named after Andrew JACKSON, who was the first territorial governor of Florida. Modern Jacksonville is a trading and financial center. It is also an important port and transportation center.

▲ *The Rouse Project is an imaginative and attractive district to help house Jacksonville's growing population.*

JAMES, Henry

Henry James (1843–1916) was a major American writer. He wrote 20 novels, including *Daisy Miller*, *The Portrait of a Lady*, and *The Ambassadors*. He also wrote plays and short stories, including the ghost story *The Turn of the Screw*. The philosopher William JAMES was his brother. From early childhood, Henry James traveled widely in Europe, and in 1876 he settled in England. Many of his books are about the conflict between American and European attitudes and moral codes.

Henry James was a tireless writer, with at least one of his books published each year from 1876 until his death in 1916. He was also a popular member of society. In the winter of 1878–1879 he accepted 140 dinner invitations.

◀ *Daisy Miller, heroine of one of Henry James's first novels, proved to be popular with American readers.*

▲ The James gang, led by Jesse James (below) and his brother Frank, staged about 25 violent robberies in Missouri. Innocent railroad workers were often killed.

William James was not afraid to express his professional opinions publicly. In 1899 he offered a description of Theodore Roosevelt, who at the time was a war hero running for president. James said that Roosevelt "gushes over war as the ideal condition of human society."

JAMES, Jesse

Jesse James (1847–1882) was a famous outlaw. He and his brother Frank were born in Missouri. They fought on the Southern side during the Civil War, with a band of guerrillas known as Quantrill's Raiders. After the war, James and Frank formed a gang that held up banks and robbed trains. When the governor of Missouri offered a reward for the James brothers, dead or alive, one of the gang shot Jesse dead. Frank James was tried but acquitted and he gave up crime.

JAMES, William

William James (1842–1910) was a famous psychologist and philosopher. His brother was the writer Henry JAMES. Born in New York City, William James earned a degree in medicine at Harvard University in 1869 and later taught there. He then became interested in how the mind works. In 1890 he wrote *The Principles of Psychology*. (Psychology is the study of the mind.) James's book *Pragmatism* (1907) contains the core of his philosophical theories.

JAMESTOWN SETTLEMENT

Jamestown was the first permanent settlement in North America. It was founded in 1607 on a small island in the James River, in Virginia. Most of the colonists died of disease or famine by the end of the year. Captain John Smith restored morale and discipline the next year by making everyone work. Smith returned to England in 1609. The following winter, 90 percent of the settlers died of starvation. But in 1612, John Rolfe (who later married POCAHONTAS) started growing tobacco. With a cash crop for sale to England, Jamestown thrived.

In 1619 the colonists were allowed to elect members to the Houses of Burgesses—the first legislative body in North America. In 1699 the capital of Virginia was moved to Williamsburg, and Jamestown was abandoned. Most of the island is now part of Colonial National Historical Park.

JANSKY, Karl

Karl Jansky (1905–1950) was an engineer. He was born in Norman, Oklahoma. In 1931, Jansky searched for the source of static that was affecting transatlantic messages. He came to the conclusion that some of the static came from outside the solar system. It was radio waves from outer space. Jansky's important discovery led to the development of radio astronomy. This field of science uses radio telescopes to study space by "listening" rather than using optical telescopes.

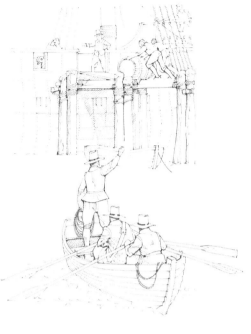

▲ Jamestown's tobacco exports kept the settlement from starvation in the early years.

JAY, John

John Jay (1745–1829) was a distinguished diplomat during the early history of the United States and the first chief justice of the U.S. Supreme Court.

Born in New York City, Jay began practicing law when he was 23 years old. He was a member of the First CONTINENTAL CONGRESS and president of the Second. After the American REVOLUTION he helped negotiate the Treaty of Paris, in which Britain recognized U.S. independence. Jay believed in a strong central government, and he wrote five of *The Federalist* papers, which urged the ratification of the U.S. CONSTITUTION.

President George WASHINGTON appointed Jay as the first chief justice of the U.S. Supreme Court. He served in that position from 1789 to 1795. In 1794, Jay was sent to England on a special mission—to avoid war with that country. The British still occupied forts in U.S. territory, and they were seizing American ships on the high seas. Under the terms of Jay's Treaty, the British agreed to leave the forts. Jay later served as governor of New York from 1795 to 1801.

▼ Jay's Treaty, signed in 1794, resolved some issues between the United States and Britain. But it did not protect American ships from being searched. This angered many Americans. It passed by a bare two-thirds majority in the Senate in 1795.

JAZZ

▶ Harlem's Cotton Club, jazz mecca of the 1920s

◀ Dizzy Gillespie is one of the world's favorite trumpet players.

Jazz is the kind of music in which players *improvise*—start with a tune and make changes in the melody and rhythm. Jazz has a *syncopated* rhythm—that is, the accent (beat) falls in unexpected places. The basis of jazz is the blues, a form of black American folk music.

Jazz developed around 1900 in NEW ORLEANS. By the 1920s this music was called Dixieland. The most important jazz musician of this era was the trumpeter and singer Louis ARMSTRONG. By the 1930s, Chicago and New York were the centers of jazz. Duke ELLINGTON, Count BASIE, and Benny GOODMAN perfected big-band jazz. Their music was often called "swing" for its inventive rhythms. The most important musician of the 1940s was saxophonist Charlie Parker. The fast tempos and complex chords and rhythms of Parker and his followers were called "bebop." Even more complex and innovative is the jazz of later musicians such as John Coltrane, Ornette Colman, and Charlie Mingus.

▲ Jazz singer Ella Fitzgerald

◀ Charlie Parker (far left), Miles Davis

Types of Jazz

Bop, or bebop, is a type of jazz played by smaller bands. Complex rhythms are played with strong feeling.

Dixieland continues the New Orleans jazz of the early 1900s. It is loud and cheerful and uses the band as a team.

Fusion, developed by musicians such as Miles Davis, combines jazz techniques with those of rock music.

Swing was the "big band" music of the 1930s and early 1940s. Soloists were backed up by repeated melodies from the band.

◄ *Louis Armstrong (trumpet) played with King Oliver's Creole Jazz Band in 1920.*

Giants of the Jazz World

Louis Armstrong (1900–1971) was an accomplished trumpet player and perhaps the greatest figure in jazz. His gruff but good-natured singing added to his popularity.

Count Basie (1904–1984) was a popular and innovative bandleader and pianist.

Bix Beiderbecke (1903–1931) was a cornetist and the greatest white jazzman of the 1920s.

Miles Davis (1926–1991) is a trumpeter who developed a soft but complex style known as "cool jazz."

Duke Ellington (1899–1974) was a bandleader and pianist who composed and arranged his own music.

Benny Goodman (1909–1986) was known as the "King of Swing." (Swing is a type of big-band jazz.)

Wynton Marsalis (1961–) is a trumpeter who is equally happy playing jazz or classical music.

Charlie Parker (1920–1955) was a brilliant saxophone player who changed the face of jazz after World War II.

▲ *Many jazz lovers consider Bessie Smith to be the greatest singer ever produced by America.*

Some of the greatest jazz musicians have led unconventional lives and received funny nicknames along the way — such as "Cannonball" Adderley, Eddie "Lockjaw" Davis, "Jelly Roll" Morton, Clarence "Pinetop" Smith, and "Fats" Waller.

◄ *Preservation Hall in New Orleans is the famous home of New Orleans jazz.*

Thomas Jefferson
Born: April 13, 1743, in Shadwell, Virginia
Education: College of William and Mary
Political party: Democratic-Republican
Term of office: 1801–1809
Married: 1772 to Martha Wayles Skelton
Died: July 4, 1826, at Monticello, Virginia

► *Jefferson's action against the Barbary pirates led to the first U.S. foreign military action.*

▼ *An architectural drawing of Monticello.*

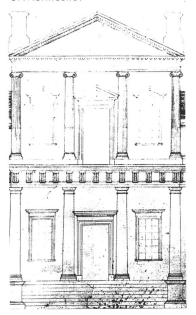

Thomas Jefferson was the third president of the United States and the main author of the DECLARATION OF INDEPENDENCE. Jefferson was talented in many areas. He was not only a politician but also a lawyer, writer, scientist, inventor, farmer, educator, and architect.

Jefferson came from a wealthy Virginia family. After serving in the CONTINENTAL CONGRESS, he was governor of Virginia and the first U.S. envoy to France. Although he opposed the adoption of the U.S. CONSTITUTION, Jefferson joined President George WASHINGTON's Cabinet as the first secretary of state (1790–1794). He often opposed the secretary of the treasury, Alexander HAMILTON, who wanted a strong central government. Jefferson and his followers formed the Democratic-Republican (later Democratic) Party. They believed in individual freedom and as little government as possible.

Jefferson was defeated in the 1796 presidential election but became vice president. In 1800 he was elected to the first of two terms as president. His most important achievement as president was the LOUISIANA PURCHASE, which doubled the size of the United States. Jefferson's biggest problem during his presidency was keeping the United States neutral in the war being waged by Britain and France.

In retirement Jefferson lived in Monticello, the house he had designed. On his tombstone he listed the three achievements he was most proud of. One was the Declaration of Independence. The other two were the founding of the University of Virginia and drafting the Statute of Virginia for Religious Freedom.

JEWS AND JUDAISM

Judaism is the oldest of the world's RELIGIONS that believe in montheism—that there is a single, all-powerful god. It is based on the Torah, the first five books of the Old Testament. In the Torah, God promises the land of Israel (also known as Palestine) to the Jewish people. He sets down the rules by which the Jews should live. The Ten Commandments are the most basic and familiar of these rules.

There are nearly 6 million Jews in the United States. They form the largest non-Christian community in the country and the largest Jewish community in the world. There are three branches of American Judaism—Orthodox, Conservative, and Reform. They differ on such customs as Sabbath observance and the dietary (kosher) laws.

The first Jews in North America arrived in New Amsterdam (now New York City) in 1654. By the mid-1700s, the Jews in the 13 colonies were enjoying greater freedom than anywhere else in the world. In 1880 there were about 250,000 Jews in the United States, mostly of German birth or extraction. Between 1881 and 1924, when immigration laws were tightened, nearly 2.4 million Jews came to the United States. Most of these were from Russia and Poland. In the 1930s and 1940s, Jewish people fled Nazi Germany. Now, however, the Jewish population is overwhelmingly native born.

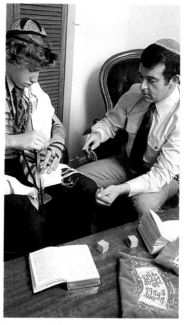

▲ Jewish boys preparing for their bar mitzvah must study scriptures and learn how to wear special religious garments such as the Teffi.

JOHNS, Jasper

Jasper Johns (1930–) is a leading American artist. His early style of art was known as pop art. This trend of the 1960s concentrated on depicting familiar, everyday objects. In Johns's work these were often letters, numerals, targets, or the American flag. His inspiration for these works came from dreams. Paint and other materials were applied thickly, so that the paintings became almost like sculptures. He also did pop art sculptures. One of these, *Painted Bronze*, consists of two beer cans.

Johns was born in Georgia and studied at the University of South Carolina. After moving to New York he worked for a while designing window displays for Tiffany's jewelry store. Johns destroyed his earliest works when he became famous in the 1950s. He also designed sets for the Merce Cunningham Dance Company.

▼ Dancers on a Plane *by Jasper Johns was part of a set he designed for the dancer Merce Cunningham in 1980.*

JOHNSON, Andrew

Andrew Johnson
Born: December 29, 1808, in Raleigh, North Carolina
Education: Self-taught
Political party: National Union
Term of office: 1865–1869
Married: 1827 to Eliza McCardle
Died: July 31, 1875, at Carter Station, Tennessee

▶ *The Civil Rights Act of 1866 made black people full U.S. citizens for the first time.*

▼ *Publications such as* Harper's Weekly *poked fun at President Andrew Johnson's planned Reconstruction of the South.*

Andrew Johnson was the 17th president of the United States. As vice president he took over the presidency when Abraham LINCOLN was assassinated in 1865. Johnson was the only president never to have gone to school. Johnson became a member of the U.S. House of Representatives, governor of Tennessee, and a U.S. senator. He was the only Southern senator who remained loyal to the Union during the CIVIL WAR. He was made military governor of Tennessee and in 1864 was elected vice president. A little more than a month after taking office, he became president.

As president, Johnson stuck rigidly to policies that treated the South gently during the RECONSTRUCTION period that followed the end of the Civil War. Congress had a majority of Republicans and wanted more drastic

measures taken. It wanted, for example, to punish the leaders of the Confederacy and give the vote to Southern blacks. Johnson vetoed (refused to approve) a number of congressional bills. He believed that the Southern states should deal with their postwar problems with little federal interference. His veto of the Civil Rights Bill in 1866 was overruled by Congress.

When Johnson dismissed the secretary of war without the approval of the Senate, Congress tried to remove him from office. This process is known as IMPEACHMENT. The impeachment failed by one vote, and Johnson finished his term of office. His major achievement was the purchase of Alaska from Russia.

In 1875, Tennessee again elected Johnson U.S. senator. He died a few months later.

JOHNSON, Lyndon B.

Lyndon B. Johnson was the 30th president of the United States. He took office in 1963 when President John F. KENNEDY was assassinated in Dallas, Texas.

A Democrat from Texas, Johnson served in Congress for 24 years. As leader of the Senate Democrats, he was a powerful political figure. In 1960 he was elected vice president as Kennedy's running mate. Johnson won the presidential election of 1964 easily. He set a record by winning 61 percent of the vote in defeating Republican Barry Goldwater.

A heavily Democratic Congress passed almost all the "Great Society" legislation that Johnson requested. First came a tax cut and a "war on poverty" to promote economic development in poor areas of the country.

Lyndon Johnson
Born: August 27, 1908, in Stonewall, Texas
Education: Southwest Texas State Teachers College
Political party: Democrat
Term of office: 1963–1969
Married: 1934 to Claudia Alta Taylor
Died: January 22, 1973, in Johnson City, Texas

◄ Lyndon Johnson signing his "Great Society" measures. These aimed to improve conditions for racial minorities, the poor, and the elderly.

▼ Lyndon Johnson was sworn in as president on board Air Force One, the presidential jet.

Other bills established the Medicare program for the elderly and increased federal funding for education and housing. There were also new IMMIGRATION and CONSERVATION measures.

Racial tensions were high at this time. The CIVIL RIGHTS movement, led by Martin Luther KING, Jr., held peaceful protests. In response, Johnson promoted measures against racial discrimination in voting, housing, employment, and public accommodations. Nevertheless, riots broke out in the black neighborhoods of many cities.

In 1965, Johnson sent U.S. troops to fight the VIETNAM WAR. After three years of bloody fighting, the Communists seemed as strong as ever. With opposition to the war growing at home, Johnson called for peace talks and chose not to run for reelection in 1968.

▲ On his way back to Montreal, Jolliet's canoe overturned and he lost his journal and maps of the area he had explored. He later redrew the maps from memory.

JOLLIET, Louis

Louis Jolliet (1645–1700) was a French Canadian explorer. In 1673 he and a priest, Father Jacques MARQUETTE, led an expedition to find the Mississippi River, which they had heard of from the Indians.

The government of New France had hoped that the Mississippi flowed westward to the Pacific Ocean. If this was the case, it would be a route to Asia. But Marquette and Jolliet's five-month journey, which followed the river by canoe as far as southern Arkansas, proved that it flowed south. From friendly Indians they learned that the Spanish occupied land farther south, and they realized that the river flowed into the Gulf of Mexico. Jolliet explored many other territories of North America.

JOLSON, Al

Al Jolson (1886–1950) was one of the most famous singers and entertainers of this century. His real name was Asa Yoelson. He was born in Russia, but his family moved to the United States when he was seven. Jolson learned English and began singing on stage when he was only 11 years old. By the time he was 25, he was one of America's highest-paid performers. In 1927, Jolson starred in *The Jazz Singer*, the first feature-length movie to have sound. His song-and-dance routine became world famous. "Swanee," "Mammy," and "April Showers," were some of his most famous songs.

▼ Thousands of copies of the sheet music to "My Mammy" were sold in the 1920s.

JONES, Bobby

Bobby Jones (1902–1971) was one of GOLF's greatest players. He won 13 major championships in the eight years that he played, but he never became a professional. Jones shocked the golfing world by winning the British Open in 1926. He was the first amateur to win that title. He won it three more times before he retired in 1930. Jones organized the Masters Tournament as a way of inviting the best players to Georgia.

JONES, John Paul

John Paul Jones (1747–1792) was a great naval hero of the American REVOLUTION. He is called the "father of the United States Navy." Jones was born in Scotland

and served on British ships. He moved to the United States in 1773.

When the Revolutionary War broke out, Jones offered his services and was commissioned an officer in the Continental Navy. Over the next six years, he scored a string of brilliant successes, capturing, sinking, and burning many British ships. His most spectacular victory took place in 1779, off the coast of England. As captain of the *Bonhomme Richard*, he captured a British man-of-war, the *Serapis*, after a four-hour battle. Jones's ship was so badly damaged that it sank two days after the battle. He and his crew sailed away in the *Serapis*.

After the war, Jones did not receive the recognition that he had expected and moved to Europe. He fell ill and died in Paris. A century later, however, he was given an appropriate grave at the U.S. Naval Academy in Annapolis.

▲ *John Paul Jones was given command of his first American ship, the sloop* Providence, *in 1776. On his first cruise with the ship he destroyed the British fisheries in Nova Scotia and captured 16 British ships.*

 ◀ *In 1779, Jones's ship the* Bonhomme Richard *captured the British ship* Serapis. *They had been so close that their riggings became entangled.*

JOPLIN, Scott

Scott Joplin (1868–1917) was a great pianist and composer of ragtime music. Joplin was born in Texarkana, Texas, where his mother had been a slave. He taught himself piano in the house of his mother's employer. By the 1890s he was a popular piano player in the bars and music halls of Missouri. Joplin played ragtime, a type of piano music with a catchy beat. His ragtime compositions, such as "Maple Leaf Rag" and "The Entertainer," are still popular today. Joplin also composed two operas. *Treemonisha* was finally produced in 1972, years after Joplin's death.

Scott Joplin published some 60 compositions, of which 41 are piano rags. During his lifetime, Joplin was never recognized as a serious composer. In 1971, interest in his music was revived, and in 1976 the Advisory Board on the Pulitzer Prizes awarded Joplin a special citation for his contribution to American music.

▲ *When Chief Joseph surrendered to the U.S. Army, he said, "My heart is sick and sad. From where the sun now stands, I will fight no more forever."*

JOSEPH, Chief

Chief Joseph (1840?–1904) was a leader of a band of NEZ PERCÉ Indians in northeastern Oregon. Beginning in 1863, when gold was discovered, whites swarmed into the area. In May 1877 the federal government ordered Chief Joseph's people to be moved. At first the chief agreed. But his people were angry, and war broke out. The Nez Percé won several victories over U.S. Army troops. But when a force of 600 men was sent to capture him, Joseph decided to retreat. He led his band of 750 people toward Canada. After a journey of 1,500 miles (2,400 km), they were forced to surrender in October 1877. Chief Joseph never saw his homeland again. He died on a reservation in the state of Washington.

JOURNALISM

Journalism is the providing of news and information for the public. It can be divided into two types. The *press*, mainly newspapers and magazines, uses accounts written by reporters to present the news. The system of news reporting on television and radio is often called the *news media*. It is part of the broadcasting industry. Big-city newspapers and national radio and television networks can afford to send reporters to cover news stories. The local press and media rely on *news services*, news-gathering organizations that supply news reports for a fee.

The best American journalism is honored by the PULITZER PRIZES. They go to outstanding examples of public service, news photography, national and international reporting, and many other fields of journalism.

JUVENILE DELINQUENCY

Juvenile delinquency is the breaking of laws by young people under the age of 18. In 1989, nearly 17 percent of all arrests were of juveniles. Juvenile delinquents are tried in juvenile courts. These courts try to help the young people rather than punish them. Juvenile delinquents who are convicted are sent to such facilities as detention centers, camps, and halfway houses. Here again the justice system tries to help them by providing education and work training. Two major causes of juvenile delinquency are poverty and broken homes.

NUMBER OF JUVENILE ARRESTS
(**in thousands**)

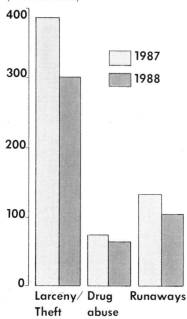

- 1987
- 1988

400
300
200
100
0

Larceny/ Theft Drug abuse Runaways

KAHN, Louis

Louis Isadore Kahn (1901–1974) was a famous architect. He was born in Estonia, now part of the USSR, but came to the United States when he was only four. He studied and lived most of his life in Philadelphia. He taught architecture at the University of Pennsylvania from 1957 until 1974. Kahn believed that the "useful" parts of buildings, such as staircases and air ducts, should be shown and not hidden. His first major work was the Yale University Art Gallery (1953).

◀ The Salk Institute in La Jolla, California, displays Kahn's love of concrete and open spaces.

KAMEHAMEHA I

Kamehameha I (1758?–1819) united the Hawaiian islands to form the Kingdom of Hawaii. He was known as Kamehameha the Great, and his birthday, June 11, is a state holiday in Hawaii.

In 1792, Kamehameha defeated a cousin in battle to gain control of most of the island of Hawaii. Between then and 1810, he gained control of the other islands. Some were conquered while others were obtained by peaceful means. Kamehameha worked very hard to make Hawaii strong and wealthy. He also tried to maintain the native customs and religious beliefs of his people. Two of Kamehameha's sons and two of his grandsons ruled Hawaii until 1872.

> **Kamehameha's formation of the Kingdom of Hawaii came at a time when other Pacific islands were falling under European control. Kamehameha called on Hawaiians to set aside their differences in order to resist the colonial threat.**

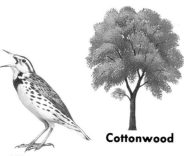

Western meadowlark

Cottonwood

Sunflower

Kansas, nicknamed the Sunflower State, is located in the very center of the United States. Farming and meat packing are two of the state's most important industries. Large farms are located in the flat central plain of Kansas. In the east there are rolling hills. The western part of the state rises up to become part of the high plains of the western United States.

Kansas produces more wheat than any other state. The wheat is stored with other grains in huge grain silos. Grains from other states are also sent to Kansas for storage. More than 200 million bushels of grain are held in the storage silos of Wichita and Topeka.

The Spanish explorer Francisco Vásquez de CORONADO was the first European to see the land that

Kansas
Capital: Topeka
Area: 81,778 sq mi (211,805 km²). Rank: 14th
Population: 2,485,600 (1990). Rank: 32nd
Statehood: Jan. 29, 1861
Principal rivers: Kansas, Republican, Smoky Hill, Arkansas, Missouri
Highest point: Mt. Sunflower, 4,039 ft (1,231 m)
Motto: *Ad Astra per Aspera* (To the Stars Through Difficulties)
Song: "Home on the Range"

Places of Interest
● The Eisenhower Center in Abilene is located at the boyhood home of President Dwight D. Eisenhower.
● Kansas Cosmosphere and Space Center, in Hutchinson, is a science museum with special exhibits on space exploration.
● Dodge City has preserved many storefronts made famous in its Wild West frontier days.

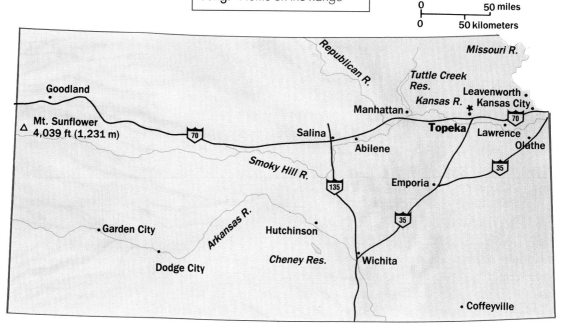

◄ Modern combines harvest the important Kansas wheat crop. Kansas is the leading state in wheat production, with about 300 million to 400 million bushels each year.

▲ A reconstruction of Texas Street gives a Wild West flavor to Old Abilene Cow Town in Abilene.

▼ The Monument Rocks are reminders that glaciers covered most of Kansas in the last Ice Age of 10,000 years ago.

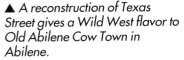

is now Kansas. He traveled there from Mexico in 1541, looking for gold. Later, the French had control over the territory. In 1803, Kansas was part of the huge parcel of land sold by the French to the United States in the LOUISIANA PURCHASE. It became a territory. In the years before the CIVIL WAR, no slaves were allowed in Kansas, so Southern states would not let it become a state. Kansas finally became the 34th state in 1861, just as the Civil War was starting.

Kansas developed quickly after the Civil War. The new railroad lines built across the United States ran through Kansas. The railroads allowed farmers to ship crops and livestock easily and cheaply. Abilene and Dodge City started out as railroad junctions for cattle trains. Today Kansas has a large aircraft industry. Automobiles are also produced there.

▲ Modern office buildings rise in downtown Kansas City.

KANSAS CITY, Missouri

Kansas City is MISSOURI's largest city, with a population of 435,146. It is on the state's western border, where the Kansas and Missouri rivers meet. A different Kansas City, in Kansas, is just across the Missouri River. Because of its river location, Kansas City has long been an important shipping center. Grain and cattle from the central Midwest are shipped through Kansas City. Huge grain elevators are used for storage of the wheat. The world price of wheat is decided in Kansas City.

Kansas City began as a trading post in 1821. It began to grow after the start of the California gold rush of 1849. Prospectors needed clothing and equipment, and Kansas City was used as their major trading center. Today Kansas City is an important industrial city. Only Detroit produces more automobiles. Meat packing and food-processing are also important industries.

KEATON, Buster

Buster Keaton (1895–1966) was an American motion-picture actor. He was best known for his silent-film comedies. His trademark was an unsmiling, deadpan expression. Keaton went into films in 1917. He had already had a successful career on the stage, having

Buster Keaton was a superb acrobat. In his films he was always a loner who triumphed over the most mind-boggling disasters.

▶ Buster Keaton's unsmiling expression in all his comedies earned him the nickname "the Great Stone Face."

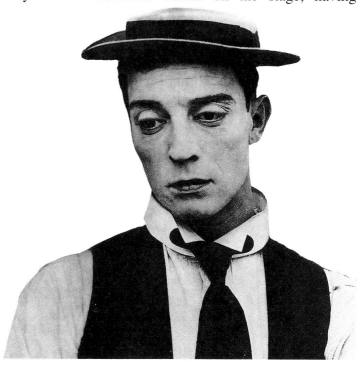

joined his parents' vaudeville act before the age of four. Keaton also wrote and directed films. His best motion pictures were *The Navigator*, *The General*, and *The Cameraman*. When sound films began to be made during the late 1920s, Keaton's success declined.

KELLER, Helen

As the result of an illness when she was not yet two years old, Helen Keller (1880–1968) became deaf and blind. Because of this, she could not speak. When Keller was almost seven, Anne Sullivan became her teacher. She taught Keller to read and write braille, a special alphabet for people who are blind. Keller eventually learned to speak also. (The story was made famous in the 1960s award-winning play and film *The Miracle Worker*.) Keller went to Radcliffe College and graduated with honors in 1904. She then devoted herself to helping other people who were blind and deaf. Among the many books she wrote are *The Story of My Life* and *Midstream: My Later Life*.

▲ *Helen Keller learned to talk from her friend and teacher Anne Sullivan. First she had to learn what talking was.*

KELLOGG, Frank

Frank Billings Kellogg (1856–1937) was prominent in both national and international politics. He was born in Potsdam, New York, and studied law. He became a U.S. senator from Minnesota in 1917. Kellogg was the U.S. ambassador to Great Britain from 1923 to 1925, and secretary of state under President Calvin COOLIDGE from 1925 to 1929. He also helped negotiate the Kellogg-Briand Pact of 1928. This international agreement to outlaw the use of war to solve international disputes was signed by 64 countries. To honor his work, Kellogg was given the Nobel Peace Prize in 1929. From 1930 he served as a judge of the Permanent Court of International Justice.

KELLY, Gene

Gene Kelly (1912–) is a dancer, singer, and actor. He is best known for his work in the lavish Hollywood musicals of the 1940s and 1950s. The dance numbers he created were enormously entertaining. They helped to reveal the characters and tell the story. Kelly's style of dance, though based on ballet, was highly athletic. (As a

The Kellogg-Briand Pact was formally known as the Treaty for the Renunciation of War. It failed in this purpose, however, because the pact did not provide a way to punish aggressors.

Unlike many other Hollywood dancers, who came from a background of vaudeville or theater, Gene Kelly has been totally involved with moviemaking. He codirected *On the Town* and *Singin' in the Rain*, two classic musicals in which he also starred.

boy in Pittsburgh he had excelled at ice hockey and other sports.) Among the best known of his films are *An American in Paris* and *Singin' in the Rain*.

In 1951, Kelly received a special Oscar for his achievements as dancer, singer, actor, choreographer, and director.

► Les Girls *gave Gene Kelly the chance to show off all his talents as a singer and dancer.*

▼ *Grace Kelly's charm and sophistication made her a favorite with movie directors and audiences alike.*

KELLY, Grace

Grace Kelly (1929–1982) was a motion-picture actress and princess of Monaco. She began her career as a stage actress in 1949. Her first film was *Fourteen Hours*. Three years later, in 1954, her performance in *The Country Girl* won her the Academy Award for best actress. During her six-year Hollywood career, she starred in 11 films. Possibly her best roles were in the Alfred Hitchcock films *Dial M for Murder*, *Rear Window*, and *To Catch a Thief*. Her other films included *High Noon*, *The Swan*, and *High Society*.

Grace Kelly gave up acting in 1956 and married Prince Rainier III, the ruler of Monaco, a small country along France's southern border. Princess Grace died as a result of an automobile accident.

KENNEDY FAMILY

The Kennedy family is one of the most famous in U.S. history. It has provided the country with a president, three senators, a congressman, a U.S. attorney-general, and an ambassador to Great Britain.

Joseph Patrick Kennedy (1888–1969) was born in Boston, the son of Irish immigrants. He married Rose Fitzgerald (1890–   ), the daughter of the mayor of Boston, in 1914. Kennedy became the country's youngest bank president when he was 25 and amassed a fortune by the time he was 30. He was ambassador to Great Britain from 1937 to 1940.

Joseph and Rose Fitzgerald Kennedy had nine children. All four sons went to Harvard University. Joseph, Jr. (1915–1944), a U.S. Navy pilot, was killed in World War II. John (1917–1963) was also a war hero. He later became a congressman, then a senator, and, in 1961, the first Roman Catholic president of the United States. He was assassinated in 1963. Robert (1925–1968) was U.S. attorney-general in his brother's Cabinet. After John's assassination, Robert was elected to the U.S. senate from New York in 1964. While campaigning for the Democratic presidential nomination in 1968, he was assassinated. Edward (1932–   ), the youngest Kennedy child, is the senior senator from Massachusetts. Joseph P. Kennedy II (1952–   ), Robert's son, was elected a congressman from Massachusetts in 1986.

▲ Robert Kennedy was campaigning for the presidency when he was assassinated in June 1968.

▲ Edward Kennedy was only 30 years old when he was elected U.S. senator from Massachusetts in 1962.

◄ The Kennedy family gathered for this photograph in November 1960, the day after John F. Kennedy (center) had been elected president.

John F. Kennedy
Born: May 29, 1917, in Brookline, Massachusetts
Education: Harvard University
Political party: Democratic
Term of office: 1961–1963
Married: 1953 to Jacqueline Lee Bouvier
Died: Nov. 22, 1963, in Dallas, Texas

▶ *On August 28, 1963, John F. Kennedy met with civil rights leaders (including Martin Luther King, Jr.) who had marched to Washington.*

▼ *First Lady Jacqueline Kennedy with Caroline and John, Jr.*

John Fitzgerald Kennedy was the 35th president of the United States and the first Roman Catholic to become president. Kennedy and his wife, Jacqueline, brought to the White House a special combination of youth and informality, glamour, and style.

John Kennedy was a hero during World War II. Later, he drew on his war record and his father's wealth and Democratic Party connections to enter politics. He was elected to the U.S. House of Representatives from Boston in 1946 and to the Senate from Massachusetts in 1952. In 1960, Kennedy became the Democratic Party nominee for president. He and the Republican nominee, Richard NIXON, held four television debates on the issues. Kennedy impressed the viewers with his intelligence and force of personality. At 43, he became the

youngest elected president, narrowly defeating Nixon.

Once in office, Kennedy stepped up the U.S. SPACE PROGRAM in order to put a man on the moon. He established the PEACE CORPS and supported CIVIL RIGHTS for black people. Kennedy also favored a government programs for the elderly and more federal aid to education. Kennedy's greatest challenge came in 1962, when the Soviet Union installed nuclear missiles in Cuba. He insisted that the missiles be removed and stopped ships from entering or leaving Cuba. The world seemed on the brink of nuclear war, but the Soviets backed down and removed the missiles.

Kennedy was assassinated on November 22, 1963, in Dallas, Texas, by Lee Harvey Oswald. Vice President Lyndon B. JOHNSON then became president.

KENT, Rockwell

Rockwell Kent (1882–1971) was an explorer and travel writer who gained greater fame as a painter and illustrator. He was born in Tarrytown Heights, New York, and studied architecture at Columbia University. He traveled to the two ends of the American continents, from Alaska to Cape Horn. He wrote and illustrated books about these and other adventures. He also illustrated books by other authors, such as Herman MELVILLE's *Moby Dick*. Kent's illustrations, often in stark black and white, were bold and eye-catching.

Rockwell Kent was a leading campaigner for world peace, even though his views were unpopular during the Cold War. He visited the Soviet Union many times and even led a committee to promote friendship between the Soviet Union and the United Sates.

◀ *A detail of Rockwell Kent's* Sundown, Greenland. *Kent's paintings were based on his own experience traveling in the polar regions.*

▼ *Stan Kenton's intelligent love of music led him to experiment constantly. The size of his band would change from almost orchestra size to just a few players.*

KENTON, Stan

Stanley Newcomb Kenton (1912–1979) was a JAZZ pianist, composer, and bandleader. He was born in Wichita, Kansas, and began playing in jazz bands in the 1930s, when he was in his twenties. He organized a band of his own in 1941. This wartime period was the era of the big bands, which played swing music such as that of Benny Goodman and Glenn Miller. Kenton's band could swing, but he preferred to experiment rather than play just one sort of music. Over the next 35 years he mixed jazz with South American and African music. His love of new sounds led him to introduce a new instrument, the mellophone, to his trumpet section. Stan Kenton's experiments helped keep jazz alive.

KENTUCKY

Kentucky coffee tree

Goldenrod

Cardinal

The state of Kentucky is located on the border between the South and the Midwest. Its nickname is the Bluegrass State. The name Kentucky comes from an Indian word meaning "land of tomorrow."

Kentucky was the first frontier for the United States. The original 13 colonies, which became the United States, were all on the Atlantic coast. People knew that there was land to the west, but the APPALACHIAN MOUNTAINS blocked the way. In 1775, Daniel BOONE blazed his way through the Cumberland Gap in the mountains of Tennessee. Settlers soon followed and cleared the forests to make farms. This new territory became the state of Kentucky. Kentucky is still an important farming state. More than 15 million acres (6 million ha) of its land are farmed. Most farms are small compared with the farms of the Midwest. Many date

---

Places of Interest
- The John James Audubon Memorial Museum, near Henderson, contains many of the naturalist's famed bird prints.
- Mammoth Cave National Park, in central Kentucky, includes the world's largest known cave system.
- The Abraham Lincoln Birthplace National Historic Site is located near Hodgenville.
- Horse farms in the "Bluegrass" region near Lexington.

Kentucky
Capital: Frankfort
Area: 39,669 sq mi (102,743 km²). Rank: 37th
Population: 3,698,969 (1990). Rank: 23rd
Statehood: June 1, 1792
Principal rivers: Ohio, Mississippi, Cumberland, Kentucky, Green
Highest point: Black Mountain, 4,145 ft (1,263 m)
Motto: United We Stand, Divided We Fall
Song: "My Old Kentucky Home"

▶ *Mammoth Cave contains almost 200 miles (320 km) of explored and mapped passages and rooms that are 200 feet (60 m) wide.*

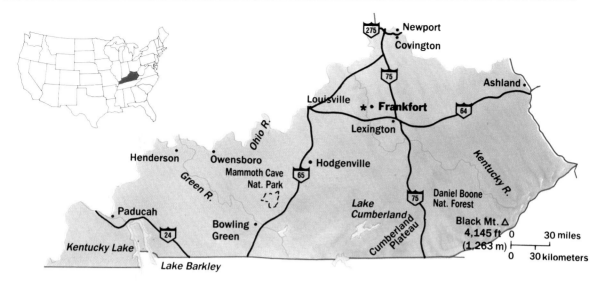

from the time of the first settlers of Kentucky. Abraham Lincoln was born on one of these small Kentucky farms. Kentucky's major crops are tobacco, corn, soybeans, and wheat.

Kentucky is the leading coal mining state. There are many mines in the hilly eastern part of the state. The coal found in this area is called anthracite. It is a hard variety and considered high-quality by the industries that use it. Among the many products made in Kentucky are whiskey, trucks and autos, food products, and chemicals.

Much of the lower land has richer soil. Horses are raised where the famous bluegrass grows. Many of the country's best racehorses come from Kentucky. The KENTUCKY DERBY, one of the world's most famous horse races, is held at Churchill Downs in Louisville.

▲ Small-scale tobacco farming is still an important part of Kentucky's agriculture.

◄ Crops and industrial goods from Louisville, Kentucky, are easily shipped from its port along the Ohio River.

383

Recent Kentucky Derby Winners	
1991	Strike the Gold
1990	Unbridled
1989	Sunday Silence
1988	Winning Colors
1987	Alysheba
1986	Ferdinand
1985	Spend a Buck
1984	Swale
1983	Sunny's Halo
1982	Gato del Sol
1981	Pleasant Colony

KENTUCKY DERBY

The Kentucky Derby is the most famous horse race in the United States. It has been held each year, on the first Saturday in May, since 1875. The race takes place at Churchill Downs in Louisville, Kentucky. The distance is 1¼ miles (2 km). Only three-year-old Thoroughbred horses can be entered, so even the best racehorses have only one chance to win. The winning horse gets more than $600,000. And the value of the horse itself rises by millions. The Kentucky Derby, along with the Belmont Stakes and the Preakness, is part of the Triple Crown of horse racing in the United States.

KERN, Jerome

The songs of Jerome Kern (1885–1945) are loved by people the world over. They include "Ol' Man River" (from his greatest musical, *Show Boat*), "Look for the Silver Lining" (from *Sally*), and "Smoke Gets in Your Eyes" (from *Roberta*).

Kern was born in New York City. He learned to play the piano from his mother and studied music in New York and Germany. His early songs were written for revivals of European operettas. He later developed a new, American style of musical comedy, with more realistic characters and songs that helped to tell the story. He also wrote music for films. His own life story is told in the film *Till the Clouds Roll By*.

▲ *Jerome Kern wrote the music for almost 50 musical comedies.*

KEROUAC, Jack

The novels of Jack Kerouac (1922–1969) are about the Beat generation of the 1950s and 1960s. These were young people who had turned their backs on conventional life. They wandered around the country in search of a good time. It was Kerouac who first called them "Beat"—meaning both "exhausted" and "beatified," or blessed.

Kerouac was born in Massachusetts, of French Canadian parents. He published his first novel, *The Town and the City*, in 1950. In his next novel, *On the Road*, Kerouac described the drifting, pleasure-seeking life he had taken up. Written in a rambling style, it made Kerouac a spokesman of the Beats. Kerouac's other novels include *The Dharma Bums* and *Big Sur*.

KING, Martin Luther, Jr.

The Reverend Martin Luther King, Jr. (1929–1968), was a Baptist minister and the main leader of the CIVIL RIGHTS movement of the 1950s and 1960s. Born in Atlanta, Georgia, King started his career as pastor of a church in Montgomery, Alabama. There, in 1955–1956, he led the successful struggle to end segregation on the city's buses.

In 1957, King helped found the Southern Christian Leadership Conference (SCLC). Its aim was to continue the civil rights struggle on a larger scale. King and the SCLC adopted a policy of nonviolent protest. They staged peaceful voter-registration drives in Selma and Birmingham, Alabama, and Albany, Georgia. They also encouraged blacks to engage in peaceful sit-ins, marches, and boycotts. Still, these civil rights workers were often the targets of violence, and King was imprisoned several times. But his courage and eloquence were a constant inspiration to blacks and whites alike.

In August 1963, King led more than 200,000 people in a march on Washington, D.C. There, at the Lincoln Memorial, he gave his famous "I have a dream" speech. In 1964, the same year that the Civil Rights Act was passed, King was awarded the Nobel Prize for Peace.

In April 1968, King traveled to Memphis, Tennessee, to help that city's mostly black workers get better working conditions. He was assassinated there by a white man, James Earl Ray. In 1983, his birthday in late January was designated a federal, legal holiday.

▼ In 1965, Martin Luther King, Jr., risked personal violence to lead a peaceful march from Selma, Alabama, to the state capitol building in Montgomery.

KING, W. L. Mackenzie

The statesman William Lyon Mackenzie King (1874–1950) was PRIME MINISTER of Canada three times. He served for a total of 21 years. King intended from childhood to enter public life. After studying at the universities of Toronto, Chicago, and Harvard, he entered the civil service as deputy minister of labor. In 1908 he was elected to Parliament. After Sir Wilfrid Laurier's death, in 1919, King became leader of the Liberal Party. King was first elected prime minister in 1921, but it was during his last term (1935–1948) that he most fully showed his qualities of leadership. During World War II, he united the country in the war effort. He then prepared the way for economic and social advances in the postwar period.

William Lyon Mackenzie King helped build Canadian pride during his 21 years as prime minister. Within Canada he supported efforts to improve relations between French speakers and English speakers. In conducting foreign policy, Mackenzie King always stressed the importance of "intermediate powers" — such as Canada — in maintaining world peace.

▼ A painted Kiowa shield shows a bear charging out from between two thunderclouds toward a row of hunters' bullets.

In 1973, Henry Kissinger shared the Nobel Peace Prize with the North Vietnamese negotiator Le Duc Tho for bringing about a cease-fire in the Vietnam War.

▼ Henry Kissinger visited the Great Wall during his 1971 trip to China. He was organizing President Nixon's famous visit the following year.

KINGFISHER

There are about 85 species of kingfishers in the world. However, only one, the belted kingfisher, is common in the United States. Some belted kingfishers migrate to Latin America in the winter. The belted kingfisher lives near rivers, lakes, and streams, and it feeds mainly on fish. During the nesting season a male and female dig a tunnel in a sandbank or claybank. They build their nest at the end of the tunnel. After the female lays its eggs, it and the male take turns sitting on them.

KIOWAS

The Kiowas were one of the Great Plains tribes. They were attracted to the plains by the horses that roamed there. Some Kiowas joined with tribes of the Athapascan culture in the southwest. They became known as the Kiowa-Apaches. Like many of the PLAINS INDIANS, the Kiowas fought to protect their land from the white settlers who began to come in great numbers. During the 1840s they fought in Texas. In the Southern Plains War of 1868–1869, the Kiowas were defeated by General Philip Sheridan, the Civil War commander. They were moved to the Indian Territory in the 1870s. Today they number about 8,000, and most live in Oklahoma.

KISSINGER, Henry

Henry Kissinger (1923–) was U.S. secretary of state from 1973 to 1977. He was largely responsible for determining U.S. foreign policy during the 1970s.

Kissinger was born in Germany. When he was 15, his family, which was Jewish, fled the Nazis and settled in New York. Kissinger fought with the U.S. Army during World War II. He then studied political science at Harvard University, receiving a Ph.D., and taught there.

Beginning in 1969, Kissinger served as national security adviser to presidents Richard NIXON and Gerald FORD. Nixon also made him secretary of state in 1973. Kissinger helped restore friendly relations with Communist China and arranged a cease-fire between the Arabs and Israelis during the 1973 war. He also negotiated a cease-fire in the VIETNAM WAR. For this, he and the North Vietnamese negotiator, Le Duc Tho, shared the 1973 Nobel Peace Prize.

KITCHEN CABINET

The term Kitchen Cabinet can refer to any informal group of presidential advisers. It originated during the presidency of Andrew JACKSON. Jackson came to rely on a group of friends and associates more than he did his official Cabinet. His political opponents did not like this. They referred to the group as the Kitchen Cabinet. One Kitchen Cabinet member, Martin VAN BUREN, went on to become president himself.

KOREAN WAR

The Korean War (1950–1953) began when North Korea, a Communist country, attacked South Korea, a pro-Western country. Nearly 3 million people died, including more than 50,000 Americans.

Korea, a peninsula in East Asia, was annexed by Japan in 1910. At the end of World War II, the Soviet Union occupied the northern part of Korea and set up a Communist government. The United States occupied the southern part and set up an anti-Communist government. In 1948 the north and the south became the independent countries of North Korea and South Korea. The boundary was formed by the 38th parallel of latitude. The government of each country claimed to be the legitimate leader of all of Korea.

On June 25, 1950, the North Korean Army invaded South Korea. Two days later the United Nations (UN) authorized its members to aid South Korea. The United

> **Stages of the Korean War**
> **June–Sept. 1950:** North Korean troops capture nearly all the peninsula.
> **Sept.–Oct. 1950:** UN troops recapture most of the Korean peninsula.
> **Nov. 1950–Jan. 1951:** Chinese and North Korean troops push south and capture Seoul (South Korea's capital).
> **Jan. 1951–July 1953:** Seoul recaptured; armistice settles border.

▼ South Korean civilians were forced to flee with few belongings after the North Koreans invaded in 1950. South Korean troops are shown here on their way to the front.

▲ *U.S. troops at the front in 1950. Late in that year they reached the Chinese border.*

States began sending troops. Sixteen other countries also sent troops. General Douglas MACARTHUR was made commander in chief of the UN forces.

Within two months, North Korean troops captured most of South Korea, including Seoul, the capital. But in September, MacArthur mounted a brilliant amphibious (a combination of land, sea and air) assault at Inchon, near Seoul, on the northwestern coast. The UN forces recaptured most of South Korea and advanced into North Korea. By November 1950 they were at the North Korean border with China. Chinese troops then entered the fighting and forced the Americans and their allies to retreat south of the 38th parallel.

Cease-fire talks began in July 1951. They dragged on for two years, as battles raged near the border. A cease-fire was finally achieved on July 27, 1953. Today there are still more than 40,000 U.S. troops in South Korea.

KOSCIUSZKO, Tadeusz

The Polish patriot and soldier Tadeusz Kosciuszko (1746–1817) is remembered in the United States for his help in the Revolutionary War. Born into the aristocracy, Kosciuszko sailed for America in 1776 and volunteered for the Continental Army. His work designing fortifications contributed greatly to several American victories, including the Battle of Saratoga (1777). At the end of the war he was made a brigadier general and given American citizenship. For the rest of his life, Kosciuszko fought to keep Poland free from Russia, Prussia (Germany), and Austria, but he was defeated in that effort. He died in exile in Switzerland.

▲ *Tadeusz Kosciuszko is often called the "Hero of Two Worlds" because of his freedom fighting in the United States and Poland.*

KU KLUX KLAN

The Ku Klux Klan was formed in 1866 by soldiers from the defeated Confederate Army. They would threaten and attack black people who were beginning to use their right to vote. Although the Klan was disbanded in 1869, it was re-formed in 1915. This time the Ku Klux Klan targets included Catholics, Jews, and immigrants, as well as black people. By 1925 it claimed membership of 4 million to 5 million. The public turned against the Klan, and new CIVIL RIGHTS laws made it harder for it to operate. Although its numbers have dwindled, the Klan is still active in some states.

◀ *Peaceful labor union demonstrations, such as this one organized by teachers, are designed to gain public support.*

LABOR UNIONS

The first nationwide labor unions in the United States, such as the Knights of Labor, were formed in the mid-1800s. They were organized by skilled workers, such as ironworkers, printers, and blacksmiths. But the labor movement really got under way in 1886, when Samuel GOMPERS organized some unions of skilled workers into the American Federation of Labor (AFL). The AFL established the process of collective bargaining to achieve better wages and working conditions.

In the late 1800s and early 1900s, there was strong opposition to organized labor. But during the DEPRESSION, people realized that unions were necessary to give workers some security. Congress passed several laws protecting the rights of unions, including the right to go on strike. In 1935, John L. LEWIS founded the Committee for Industrial Organization (later renamed the Congress of Industrial Organization, CIO). It was generally more aggressive in its policies than the AFL. In 1955 the AFL and CIO merged.

In recent years, new groups of workers—including migrant farm workers—have become unionized. But membership as a whole has declined. Today, only about 18 percent of the work force belong to labor unions.

▲ *David Dubinsky, seen here at a 1957 rally, was a labor leader in the clothing industry for more than 25 years.*

LACROSSE

Lacrosse is a sport in which team members use a stick with a net on the end to throw a ball into their opponents' goal. There are ten players on each team. Lacrosse was invented by the Indians of Canada, where it remains a national sport. The National Lacrosse Association of Canada and the U.S. Intercollegiate Lacrosse Association are important governing bodies. In the United States, the University of Maryland and John Hopkins University are among the top teams.

LAFAYETTE, Marquis de

A French aristocrat, the Marquis de Lafayette (1757–1834) fought with the American colonists in the Revolutionary War and later played a leading role in the French Revolution.

In July 1777 the young Lafayette went to Philadelphia and volunteered for duty. He was commissioned a major general and fought in several important battles. In 1779 he helped persuade the French king, Louis XVI, to send aid to the American colonists. As commander of an army in Virginia, Lafayette contributed significantly to the victory at Yorktown.

When Lafayette returned to France in 1782, he tried to steer his country's own revolution in a moderate course. He was unpopular with those who wanted more extreme changes. Lafayette played an important part in the French Revolution of 1789 and later sat in the French Chamber of Deputies.

▲ *Bagataway, the original Indian version of lacrosse, gave young braves a chance to demonstrate their skill.*

▼ *In the siege of Yorktown in 1781, Lafayette sent a courier to his friend General George Washington with important news of the British defenses.*

LA FOLLETTE, Robert M.

Robert La Follette (1855–1925) was a Wisconsin political leader and reformer. He served as a U.S. congressman, state governor, and U.S. senator. A Republican, La Follette belonged to his party's progressive wing. He fought for workers' rights and against big business. He tried to check the power of the railroads and other large corporations and to have fair taxation. The reform measures introduced by La Follette became known as the Wisconsin Idea.

In the U.S. Senate (1906–1925), La Follette continued to fight against "special interests." He also opposed U.S. entry into World War I and the League of Nations. He broke with the Republican Party in 1924 and was nominated for the presidency by the Progressive Party. La Follette received 5 million votes, but he won only the electoral votes of his home state.

▲ *Robert La Follette's campaigns against "big business" and corruption earned him the nickname "Battling Bob."*

LAKES

There are more lakes in the northern part of the United States than in the southern part. Many of these were formed by melting glaciers, which at one time covered large areas of the northern United States. The GREAT LAKES were partly formed in this way. Minnesota has about 11,000 glacial lakes. Lakes often form in limestone areas, when water drains into deep hollows in the ground. Lake County, Florida, has more than 1,400 of

▼ *The wooded shores of Lake Tahoe are only a short drive away from Carson City, Nevada, and California's Squaw Valley ski resort.*

Largest Lakes in
North America (sq mi/km²)
Superior (31,820/82,414)
Huron (23,010/59,596)
Michigan (22,400/58,016)
Great Bear
(12,000/31,080)
Great Slave
(11,170/28,930)
Erie (9,930/25,719)
Winnipeg (9,094/23,553)
Ontario (7,520/19,477)

these. The deepest lake in North America, Oregon's Crater Lake, is more than one third of a mile (half a kilometer) deep. It was formed by rainwater collecting in the crater of an extinct (dead) volcano. Lake Superior, one of the Great Lakes, is the largest lake in North America and the second largest in the world. North America's largest salt lake, GREAT SALT LAKE, is only about 15 feet (4.5 m) deep. Lake Mead, in Nevada and Arizona, is the United States' largest artificial lake. It was formed by the building of Hoover Dam on the COLORADO RIVER.

LAND, Edwin Herbert

The physicist Edwin Herbert Land (1909–1991) invented the Polaroid camera. This camera takes and prints photographs in a minute or so. The invention grew out of Land's earlier studies, at Harvard University, in the polarization of light. In 1932 he invented a material that reduced glare. Land founded the Polaroid Corporation in 1937. Some of its products, such as sights for anti-aircraft guns and night-adaptable goggles, were used during World War II. The Polaroid camera appeared in 1947. A model that takes color photographs was introduced in 1963.

▲ *Even the first Polaroid Land cameras were lightweight and designed for everyday use.*

LANGLEY, Samuel Pierpont

Samuel Langley (1834–1906) was the first person to build a successful heavier-than-air flying machine. Langley was a civil engineer and architect. He later

▶ *Langley's pilotless aircraft of 1896 was a forerunner of the Wright brothers' airplane seven years later.*

taught mathematics and became a professor of physics and astronomy at the University of Pittsburgh. He was especially interested in solar activity and its effect on the weather. Langley also made important studies on the nature of flight. His flying machine was first tested in 1896, in a flight over the Potomac River. It weighed 26 pounds (9.7 kg) and was powered by a steam engine. Langley also worked on a manned aircraft but lost this race to the Wright brothers. He served as secretary of the Smithsonian Institution from 1887 until his death.

LANGMUIR, Irving

Irving Langmuir (1881–1957) was an important scientist of this century. He was born in Brooklyn and studied at Columbia University and in Germany. Langmuir worked at the General Electric Research Laboratory from 1909 to 1950. There he did research in many areas. He studied how chemicals react at high temperatures and low pressure. His findings led to the development of the gas-filled tungsten lamp. His work also led to the improvement of electron tubes. Langmuir also invented an atomic hydrogen welding torch and discovered how to produce rain by seeding clouds with dry ice. Langmuir received the Nobel Prize for chemistry in 1932 for his studies that were related to work with the tungsten bulb. He also helped to develop radar in World War II.

LANGUAGE

English is the main language spoken in North America, even though only about 15 percent of U.S. citizens have English ancestors. In Quebec and some other parts of Canada, French is the main language of a majority of people. Mexicans, along with most other Latin Americans, speak Spanish.

Many Indians and Inuits (Eskimos) still speak their native languages. When the Europeans first arrived in North America, they found hundreds of tribes speaking a variety of languages. By the 1800s, many of these languages had died out.

Today, most U.S. immigrants (people coming to live in the United States) come from developing countries, and English is not their first language. Some people believe that education for these people should be *bilingual* — in their own language as well as in English.

▼ *Some of Irving Langmuir's later experiments developed "cloud seeding," or using chemicals to promote rain.*

In different parts of the United States, a long sandwich filled with cold cuts, onions, tomatoes, or other ingredients is known as a "hero," "submarine," "grinder," "torpedo," "hoagy," "wedge," or even "spuky." These words are called regional variations of American English.

There are more than half a million words in a large English dictionary. Most people use fewer than 10,000.

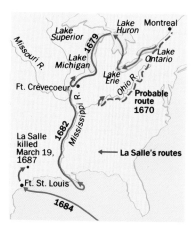

▲ La Salle's expeditions, like those of Lewis and Clark 120 years later, followed major rivers into the heart of the continent.

LARDNER, Ring

Ring Lardner (1885–1933) was a well-known sports journalist and writer of humorous short stories. He was born in Niles, Michigan, and got his first job as reporter on the *South Bend Times*, a newspaper in Indiana. He soon moved to Chicago where he worked as a reporter. Lardner's baseball stories for the *Chicago Tribune* were so popular that they were sold to other newspapers around the country. The *Saturday Evening Post*, a magazine based in New York, began to use Lardner's stories on baseball and ordinary life. He also published several collections of his stories and short plays.

LA SALLE, Robert Cavelier, Sieur de

The explorer Robert Cavelier, Sieur de La Salle (1643–1687), was the first European to travel the length of the Mississippi River. La Salle was born in France and went to Canada at the age of 23. Having made friends with local Indians, he made several journeys with them, exploring as far as present-day Wisconsin. In February 1682 he led a party of French and Indians down the Mississippi. Arriving at the Gulf of Mexico on April 9, 1682, he claimed the whole Mississippi Basin for France and named it Louisiana, for King Louis XIV. In 1684, La Salle sailed again to the Americas to start a colony there. But the expedition was beset by disasters, and La Salle was killed by mutineers.

▼ On April 9, 1682, La Salle reached the mouth of the Mississippi River. He claimed all the land in the Mississippi Basin for France, calling it Louisiana.

LAUREL AND HARDY

Stan Laurel (1890–1965) and Oliver Hardy (1892–1957) formed one of the best-loved comedy teams of this century. Laurel was born in England, Hardy in Harlem, Georgia. Eventually they both went to Hollywood. Between 1926 and 1952 they made over 60 short movies and 27 full-length features. Laurel played a shy, bumbling, rather stupid man. Hardy ("Ollie") was his fat, pompous friend. Their comedy stems from things going out of control, the tension between the two friends, and finally something unexpected happening to save them. Some of their best-known films are *Babes in Toyland*, *Sons of the Desert*, and *Blockhead*.

Between 1926 and 1950, Laurel and Hardy made over 200 slapstick films. One of them, *The Music Box*, won an Academy Award as best comedy short subject. The fat Ollie is perhaps best remembered for his long-suffering glances at the camera.

◄ *Stan Laurel wrote and directed some of the duo's best material, but his contributions were rarely credited.*

LAURIER, Sir Wilfrid

Sir Wilfrid Laurier (1841–1919) was the first French Canadian PRIME MINISTER of Canada. Born in a farming community in the province of Quebec, Laurier was educated by both French- and English-speaking teachers. Later he studied law at McGill University in Montreal. Laurier was elected to the Canadian House of Commons in 1874 as a member of the Liberal Party. He became prime minister in 1896 and served until 1911. Laurier successfully promoted the settling of the western territories and the expansion of the railroad system. Although he admired Britain, he resisted any moves to strengthen the ties between that nation and his own. Throughout his career, Laurier worked for harmony between the French and the British populations, and closer trade links with the United States. In later years, his moderate policies were attacked by extremists on both sides, and he was forced to retire in 1911.

▼ *The election of the Roman Catholic and French-speaking Sir Wilfrid Laurier as prime minister helped strengthen Canadian unity.*

Lawrence's cyclotron

Dee

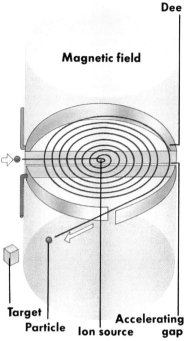

Magnetic field

Target
Particle **Ion source**
Accelerating gap

▲ *Ernest O. Lawrence's cyclotron was soon nicknamed the "atom smasher."*

Some Important Laws in U.S. History
Northwest Ordinance (1787): set out how growing territories could become new states.
Interstate Commerce Act (1887): created the first federal "watchdog", the Interstate Commerce Commission.
Income Tax Act (1913): established the federal income tax still used.
Social Security Act (1935): set up an old-age pension scheme and unemployment insurance.
Civil Rights Act (1964): banned discrimination in employment, public accommodations, and other areas.

LAWRENCE, Ernest O.

Ernest Orlando Lawrence (1901–1958) was an important physicist. Born in Canton, South Dakota, he began working on atomic energy before World War II. While at the University of California at Berkeley, he was awarded the 1939 Nobel Prize for physics for the invention and development of the cyclotron. Lawrence continued working on the atom and was involved in several major discoveries. In 1957, in recognition of all his work, the U.S. Department of Energy gave him the Enrico Fermi Award. The Lawrence Berkeley Laboratory and the Lawrence Livermore Laboratory are named for him. These centers for nuclear research are operated by the University of California.

LAWS AND LEGAL SYSTEM

Laws are rules that govern society. In the United States, written laws (or statutes) are made by representative assemblies, such as the U.S. CONGRESS, state legislatures, and city councils. In addition, executive and administrative branches of government may issue administrative acts that have the effect of laws. And courts, through decisions in individual cases, also establish rules. Such rules are sometimes called case law.

There are two basic kinds of law—civil and criminal. Civil law generally deals with disputes between individuals. For example, someone who does not live up to the terms of a contract can be sued in a civil court. Criminal laws are designed to protect the entire community. A person who breaks a criminal law—by robbing a bank, for example—faces trial in a criminal court.

The court system in the United States consists of federal and state courts. The U.S. SUPREME COURT is the highest federal court and the highest court in the country. It hears appeals of cases that were tried in federal courts and the highest state courts. There are 94 federal district courts.

State courts are independent of the federal courts. The highest state court is usually called a supreme court. Other state courts include appellate courts and courts of general trial jurisdiction. There are also county and municipal courts. Along with courts, police departments and government agencies such as the FEDERAL BUREAU OF INVESTIGATION enforce laws.